I'm Just Getting Started

I'm Just Getting Started

Baseball's Best Storyteller on Old School Baseball, Defying the Odds, and Good Cigars

Jack McKeon and Kevin Kernan

TRIUMPH
BOOKS
CHICAGO

Library of Congress Cataloging-in-Publication Data

McKeon, Jack.
   I'm just getting started : Baseball's Best Storyteller on old school baseball, defying the odds, and good cigars / Jack McKeon and Kevin Kernan.
     p. cm.
   ISBN 1-57243-711-1
    1. McKeon, Jack. 2. Baseball managers—United States—Biography. 3. Conduct of life. I. Kernan, Kevin, 1953– . II. Title.

GV865.M31235A3 2005
796.357'092—dc22
[B]

                           2004065923

This book is available in quantity at special discounts for your group or organization. For further information, contact:

Triumph Books
601 South LaSalle Street
Suite 500
Chicago, Illinois 60605
(312) 939-3330
Fax (312) 663-3557

Printed in U.S.A.
ISBN-10: 1-57243-711-1
ISBN-13: 978-1-57243-711-1
Design by Patricia Frey

To Carol, Kristi, Kelly, Kori, Kasey, Zachary, Kellan, Avery, Korney, Kenzie, Braylee, Mallory, Berkley, and Presley for all their support and love through the years.

—Jack McKeon

For Anne, Kelly Anne, Casey James, and Corey Michael, my championship team.

—Kevin Kernan

Contents

I'm Just Getting Started

CHAPTER 1

Don't Move the Wrecker

've been fired six times. That's not bad. The way I figure it, that's once every 12 years. Hell, I'm only 74.

Smoking cigars and staying in shape are important to me, so I take a few puffs and I work out every day. Five hours before the game you'll see me walking around the ballpark with that cigar in my hand, walking two or three miles, doing it my way.

One day in the spring of 2003 I was working out at the YMCA back home in Elon, North Carolina, and I noticed this young gentleman bouncing a basketball. He had to be 77 or 78 years old, and we got to talkin'. He told me the North Carolina Senior Games were coming up and said, "I'm with the senior softball and basketball teams. We need another player. Can you play?"

"OK," I said. "I can handle both of those. I'll help you out. How old are these guys we're playing?"

He said, "Seventy-two and above."

"OK, but I'm not going to hurt one of these guys if I hit them with a softball, am I?"

"No, no, they know what they're doing," he said.

"How long do you practice?"

"About an hour, some of these guys can't go too long," he said. "We practice on Tuesday and Thursday nights."

I laughed and told him my grandson played baseball on those nights. I couldn't go, but I didn't need the practice. I'd be all right. *Sign me up*, I thought, *this old catcher can still play a little.*

"Hey, when are those Senior Games?" I asked.

"August," he told me.

You know, I never did show up. Something came up. I had to go back to managing in the Major Leagues with the Florida Marlins . . . and win the World Series against the Yankees. As for that old guy back in North Carolina, it turned out that his team won the championship, too. They didn't need me after all, but the Marlins sure did.

Three days after that World Series, I signed a one-year extension. Then, after that season, I signed another extension. I don't know how long I can manage, but in my mind I'm just getting started. Casey Stengel went to 75. If I decide to stay, I won't turn 75 until the 2006 season, so I have two more seasons to go to tie Casey. I don't think I can catch Connie Mack. He went all the way until 88. I don't think I want to do that.

My wife Carol is the happiest one of all now that I'm back in the dugout. She said, "Jack, you drove me crazy being at home after being away all those years. The best thing about having you back managing is that I get the TV clicker back. That and shopping."

When Carol found out we were going to the White House to meet with President Bush after beating the Yankees, she raised her champagne bottle in the manager's office of the visiting clubhouse at Yankee Stadium and offered this toast, "Yeah! More shopping!"

Carol likes to shop as much as I like to manage. And after 55 years in the pro game, I like to manage a certain way. Too many players today are coddled. I don't play favorites, but I will bend a little, that's something I learned how to do. Darn right I'm old style, it works. You have fun, but you play hard. Too many managers want robots out there. You've got to give the players some freedom to think on their feet. You can't call every pitch and then expect your pitchers to know how to get out of jams.

I took over the Marlins on May 11, 2003. One game soon after, the guys were horsing around in the dugout, and I blew my stack. "Look at you guys," I screamed. "You guys talk the talk, but you don't know how to walk the walk. You're a bunch of babies."

They rallied to win that game and as they came back into the clubhouse they were yelling, "We walked the walk." I knew at that moment that we had something going.

Another lesson I've learned as a manager is you can't be afraid to make the tough decision. Early in my career as a manager, I'd worry about what the writers or the owners said. I wouldn't have done it this way before, but now I've got the guts to do it. I've learned to manage my way. Like a lot of people, I've gotten smarter with age.

Now I've got my first World Series ring. And it's a big, beautiful one, the biggest of all time. Our owner, Jeffrey Loria, knows how to do things right.

Managing a team is really about managing people, and it's all I ever wanted to do. From the time I was 12 years old in South Amboy, New Jersey, I was managing a baseball team. I'd set up the roster, set the schedule, and arrange the transportation.

My father, his first name was Aloysius but we called him Bill, was in the garage, taxi, and wrecking business. He supplied the bus for the games and sponsored us: we were called the "McKeon's Boys Club." It was a great setup for me. In the winter, we practiced in the garage.

We hung chicken wire over the windows and lights so nothing would get broken when we knocked the baseball around. This was in the forties, so if you think about it, I had the first indoor baseball facility and batting cage. I was ahead of my time even back then.

At night, we practiced near the traffic cloverleaf, where there was a grassy area and the lights from the highway gave us enough light to hit by. We'd play baseball day and night, summer and winter. It was never too cold to go hit.

When I wasn't playing sports, I was up in the garage, hanging out and helping my dad or driving a wrecker (even though I was underage). The garage is where I got a real education, the best kind of education, an education in life's lessons.

My father taught me how to deal with people, business smarts, and street smarts. I learned a lot just watching him operate. And the man could operate. I saw the way he could manipulate the city council, the police, and the business leaders in town. I saw how shrewd he was.

He was one tough SOB.

One New Year's Eve there was a three-car accident out on Route 35. There was no assignment for the wreckers—it was first come, first served. We got to the scene first, and then two other companies came by. The cop on the scene gave two of the cars to the wrecking company that brought two wreckers, and the other car was given to the other guy. My father didn't get any. He was shut out.

He looked at me and said, "We're going to city hall."

He pulled right in front of city hall in the circle—right in front of the steps where all the police cars have to go through—and parked the wrecker right there. He blocked the driveway so nobody could get past. Then he went inside and told the cops, "I dare you to move that wrecker." He walked out, and we went home.

The next morning the chief of police called. I answered the phone, and the chief asked, "Where's your father?"

"In bed," I said.

"Would you have him call me right away? I want him to move the wrecker."

"He ain't gonna move that wrecker," I said.

Later on, the chief called again, and this time my father answered the phone. He told the chief, "Yeah, I'll move the wrecker—when you put it in writing that I get every wreck in South Amboy."

They did just that, and he went down and moved the wrecker. That was the first big deal I ever saw. Anyone else they would have locked up, but my father had a legitimate gripe. That's when I learned, if you're right, you go for it. You don't move the wrecker.

The baseball business is just like dealing with the city council. Instead of councilmen and councilwomen, I got ballplayers, management, and umpires. The biggest thing I learned from my father was to never give up on a deal. He kept working until he got what he wanted, whether it was a taxi route with the school system or a deal with the Pennsylvania railroad during the war hauling railroad workers to trouble spots.

I've done it all and I've been everywhere. I handled the books for my father's taxi business, I handled the food stamps, the gas stamps, and all the regulations. I learned by doing.

I've had all kinds of jobs. I opened the first sports bar back in the fifties in Burlington, North Carolina. I taught school; pumped gas; drove the wrecker and a taxi; fixed cars; delivered mail; sold tires, TVs, and refrigerators; was a basketball referee; and worked the night shift in a hosiery mill. I've been in the Air Force, where I played baseball and I became a sharpshooter, medal and all, even though I never went to the range. In 1951 I managed the baseball team that won the Air Force Championship. I played baseball all over the place and hit three ways: righty, lefty, and seldom.

I've managed everywhere from Missoula, Montana, to Puerto Rico.

I've been a GM. I built the Padres team that won the club's first pennant in 1984, beating the Cubs back then just like the Marlins beat them in 2003. And I've always been a scout. People ask me, "Jack, how do you do it? How do you stay so young? How do you have so much fun? How did you become the oldest manager to ever win the World Series?"

I do it by just being myself, by not being a phony. And I've been blessed in so many ways.

I've been able to meet Presidents H. W. and George W. Bush, Nixon, and Carter, and I've received telegrams from Presidents Reagan and Nixon, all because of baseball. Baseball owes me nothing, but I sure owe a lot to baseball.

Most of all, I'm here to tell people the game is never over, it's just like Yogi Berra said, it ain't over till it's over. I first saw Yogi in 1947 with the Newark Bears. Who knew we'd both be still working on a baseball field more than half a century later? Every spring training, Yogi is there with the Yankees. You gotta keep plugging along. Persistence is the key to success. When you look back and see my career, it was a carbon copy of persistence.

For every disappointing thing, something positive came after it. Every time I got fired, I eventually ended up getting a better job until one day I'm named Manager of the Year with the Reds in 1999 and then I'm winning the World Series with the Marlins four years later. The reason for that is my attitude. The same goes in business, if you're fired or something goes wrong, it's not the end of the world. I always thought there are people in a lot worse shape than I am. And I never put my failures onto someone else.

Your attitude determines your altitude.

The first time I was supposed to get a managing job, the league folded, but I didn't quit. I finally did get a managing job at Fayetteville, I got hurt, I got fired again, I went out and scouted, then I got another managing job, this time at Missoula. I kept getting fired and I kept bouncing back. I always knew how to get a job—just keep pounding away like a salesman. You've got to sell yourself.

How do you do that? You've got to keep making contacts and keep coming back and beating the doors down until someone opens the door for you. It's like my old Oakland A's owner Charlie Finley used to say, "When Mr. Opportunity knocks. Open up the door and say, C'mooooooon in!"

You gotta have fun. You gotta laugh. Just the other day I called up my owner, Jeffrey Loria, disguised my voice, and told him it was President Bush's secretary calling. He thought it really was, and when I finally told him it was me, he laughed and said, "You got me, Jack."

I sometimes call the ticket office, change my voice, and see if I can get a discount on three thousand tickets for the Cub Scouts, the Girl Scouts, or the Boy Scouts. It takes the pressure off when you can have a good laugh.

Even walking down the street you can have fun. I was in the minors in 1969, in Oklahoma City, and Bill Beck, the team's broadcaster and traveling secretary, and I went to get something to eat after a ballgame. We were walking down the street and kept getting stopped by panhandlers. After the third panhandler came by, I figured it was time to have a little fun. The next guy came up to me and asked for money. I grabbed him by the shirt and said, "Look buddy, I'm working this side of the street, get your tail on the other side." The guy hustled over to the other side of the street.

You run into all kinds of situations managing. One winter in the seventies I was managing in Puerto Rico. The team wasn't very good, but they could cook. In the middle of the game I smelled something fishy, and there in the back of the dugout, a bunch of players were cooking crabs and fish. I soon made short order cooks of those players.

Every single day in the minors and in winter ball I had fun. It's a good thing I took that approach because it was 25 years before I stepped foot on a major league field. I started in pro ball in 1949 and didn't make it to the majors until 1973 as manager of the Royals. Then came major league managing jobs with the A's, Padres, Reds, and, 30 years after getting my first major league managing job, I got the job with the Marlins. Then all my baseball dreams came true.

You've got to have faith. I go to church every day. You keep moving, you keep going forward.

The best thing about all this is that it has been a real plus for all the senior citizens out there. You should see the letters I get. People say I've been an inspiration to them. They say they've gotten up out of the chair they've been sitting in just watching TV and have gone out, gotten a job, and are having fun again with their lives. That's what you gotta do. I can't sit on no rocking chair on a porch.

I can't sit and watch TV. I get ticked off sitting in that chair. But every day when I wasn't working I watched all the major league games I could at home in North Carolina, just to stay in touch. Then one night in May of 2003 around 10:45, the phone rings. It's the Marlins. They want me to come down to Florida. They want to talk a little baseball philosophy with me. At the time, I had no idea I would become manager.

The only thing I was sure of was that in this meeting, I was going to be myself. Through the years I've learned that you have to be yourself. It's the only way to survive in baseball. So when I went down to meet Jeffrey Loria, I went down there in a very businesslike way to discuss the philosophies of the organization. To me, I was just giving him a scouting report, being as helpful as I could possibly be.

When I left that meeting I said, "Thank you *Jerry*. It was a nice meeting. I enjoyed talking with you." Later, he told my old friend Bill Beck, who was and still is the traveling secretary of the Marlins, "Well, I know one thing, Jack sure wasn't trying to impress me. He didn't even know my name." But something must have impressed him because they called me back two nights later. I was managing in the big leagues again.

John Boggs, who helps in my business deals, said it best. "Jack does it his way," he said. "If Frank Sinatra were alive, he'd love Jack."

Regardless of your age, keep fighting. Don't give up. You might think you're too old or too poor or too sick to go on, but if you have faith, anything is possible. Look at me, I was out of work for three years, 72 years old and all signed up for the North Carolina Senior Games, and a few months later I've got the biggest World Series ring ever made.

If this job didn't come along, I would have managed in a rookie league. It's like I tell kids when I go out to the schools: you can be whatever you want to be. I still feel that way at 74. If it doesn't work today, keep at it. Don't quit. It might work tomorrow.

Don't ever give up.

Don't move the wrecker.

CHAPTER 2

Blowin' Smoke

The cigar is my trademark. People wouldn't know it's me if I didn't have my cigar. They even gave away this Jack in the Box figure one night at Pro Player Stadium, a little toy where I pop up with a cigar. They had forty-one thousand fans that night.

I've been on the cover of *Cigar Aficionado*, so I must know something about cigars.

Padron Cigars are my favorite, and I don't smoke anything but the Anniversary Series. They are the best cigars I've ever smoked and they're made right here in Miami. Jorge Padron is president of the company. I started out smoking Tampa Nuggets, two for 15 cents, but now I've graduated to Padrons. When we went to the White House, I even gave President George W. Bush some Padrons. We had a great time.

When I go for my walk around the ballpark each day, I carry two cigars. I always carry a backup. I have to hide in the tunnel to light them. Most of the time it's a one-cigar walk, but at home in Florida I start around 11:30 and it can be a two-cigar walk. People get a big kick out of seeing me walking around the field with puffs of smoke trailing behind me.

When I was in New York to do the Letterman show after we won the World Series, I didn't keep a cigar in my hotel room, I kept one on the street. That's what I usually do. I found a good hiding place for it right in front of the hotel where they were doing some construction work. I stuck it right in a scaffolding pipe, a perfect fit. Whenever I wanted a smoke, I went out on the street, pulled my cigar out of the pipe, lit up, and took a few puffs.

When the Marlins are home, I go to St. Matthew's Church every morning in Hallandale Beach. I set my stogie on a metal post just before I walk in the door and pick it up on the way out, after I've made sure to bless myself.

I started smoking cigars in 1949 and never stopped. That was my first year in pro baseball. We could never smoke or drink around my father. So once I got down to Greenville, Alabama, that year without my father around, I started smoking those Tampa Nuggets. I'd come home during the off-season and I wouldn't smoke, even though my father was a big cigar smoker. I didn't want to take the chance of smoking in front of him.

There used to be a big White Owl cigar factory in our town, and a friend would bring my father a bunch of the seconds. My father always had three boxes of White Owls around the garage and he smoked those all the time. About three years after I was in pro ball, I finally started smoking in front of him. I was shocked when nothing happened. He didn't say a word, so I kept smoking.

I always found that smoking a cigar is a good icebreaker. People want to talk to you about cigars, and for me now, it's part of my identity. I'm convinced cigars help keep me healthy.

I've always said I've been blessed, that the Good Lord is looking out for me. In 1950, for example, I broke my ankle sliding into second base in Gloversville, New York. They told me to go home on a Friday, but I decided to stay until Sunday because there was so much pain in my ankle I didn't want to get on a train. That Friday night there was a munitions blast in South Amboy that killed 33 people near the train station. The train I was going to take home would have pulled into South Amboy just a couple of minutes before the explosion. I could have been killed.

South Amboy was a great place to grow up. We lived on John Street. My younger sister, Marge Gorczyca, still lives there, right across the street from a ballfield they named after me.

I grew up idolizing Allie Clark, a local guy who played for the Yankees. Allie still lives in South Amboy, and he said one of the nicest things about me when the Marlins won the World Series. The *Star-Ledger* did a story about my hometown and talked to Allie, who said, "We were always proud of Jack, even before he got to the World Series. He was always nice to people. That's the main thing I liked about him. I respect the man because he never forgot anyone. He never ignored anyone in this town."

I've always treated people that way because that's the way Allie Clark treated people. I learned from him. I just hope that we—me, the O'Brien twins, Johnny and Eddie, who played for the Pirates, and Allie Clark—accomplished what we set out to do: to play the game right and be an inspiration for some of the young kids to follow in our footsteps. I think we did that.

The New Jersey sportswriters gave me an award this past year, and it was as if the whole state was there behind me. I also got inducted into the New Jersey Hall of Fame. That's something I never dreamed of doing growing up, but there I am with Vince Lombardi, Bill Parcells, Phil Rizzuto, Bobby Thomson, and Phil Simms. I've never forgotten my Jersey roots and never will.

It didn't start out so good, though. Even though I was a pro ballplayer, it made no difference to my father. I still had to work for him. He didn't look at me as a professional ballplayer but as his kid, and work needed to be done. One year I came home and went right to work, picking up a fare, a guy named Freddie, going from one bar to another.

Freddie was pretty drunk, and when we got to the bar he jumped right out of the cab. I thought he was jumping the fare and I didn't want to have to go back to my dad without the money, so I ran out and grabbed at Freddie. As I grabbed him, Freddie raised his arm. I thought he was going to hit me so I decked him. Boom! He flew right across the hood of the car, bounced up, and ran into the bar like a jackrabbit.

The next day I was working in the shop and my father told me he wanted to introduce me to somebody. Who did he introduce me to? Freddie. "Don't worry about Freddie, Jack," Dad said. "He's on a tab. He keeps track of what he owes me and pays me at the end of the month."

Lucky for me, Freddy didn't remember who hit him the night before. He thought it happened in the bar, so I told him, "Gee, Freddie, you were fine when I dropped you off."

That's the kind of breaks I've gotten my whole life. I've been lucky. Managing the Florida Marlins at my age is the greatest opportunity in the world and I love it. I am especially thankful to Jeffrey Loria.

People often ask why I start my day at 6:30 in the morning during spring training, or how I can stay all day and night during the season. Well, that's who I am. I've always come early to the ballpark. When I was the GM and the manager in San Diego, I would come in about 8:00 in the morning and I'd stay until 1:00 in the afternoon as the general manager, then I would go downstairs to be the manager, change into my uniform, and let Bill Beck, my assistant GM, run the show. After the game I'd put my general manager's suit back on and stay until about 1:00 in the morning.

The ballpark is my home. If I had never married Carol, I would have made myself a little apartment in the clubhouse. Through the years I've learned some pretty important things in the clubhouse. Probably the most important thing is to go with your heart, don't worry about what other people think about your decision. Make your decision based on what you think is best.

Everybody was surprised when I went with pitcher Josh Beckett on only three days' rest in Game 6 of the World Series against the Yankees. What happened? The kid threw a masterpiece, we won the game 2–0 and the Series. There's no doubt the baseball angels were with me all that season with the moves I made—and I think those angels were smoking cigars.

From the day I got this job I believed I could turn this club around and make it a winner. There was a lot of talent here; it just had to be pointed in the right direction. I felt that team could go to the World Series and that is exactly what happened.

I've always had fun being around the game. After I got fired by the Padres in 1990, I could have sat around and felt sorry for myself and just collected a paycheck (because I was still under contract), but I wanted to be around the game.

There was a new Little League starting up not too far from our house in Scripps Ranch. My wife Carol wanted me out of the house anyway. She was used to me going to the ballpark early and letting her do her thing. This wasn't a typical Little League; it was called the Challenger League. It was kids with disabilities who wanted to play baseball. They were helped out by their "buddies," kids in the regular

Little League. The buddies would push the wheelchairs or help guide the players to make a play or run the bases. I started going up there to help out, being a buddy, doing whatever I could.

It was so much fun to be around those kids. They didn't care that I used to manage the Padres, they were just happy to have the chance to play baseball. I've never forgotten that. Those kids were having the time of their lives on the ballfield, and that's always been my approach. Have fun and don't be afraid to do things a little differently. Baseball is supposed to be fun. People always forget that.

I remember one time when I was managing in Omaha and our hitters were swinging at pitches that weren't even close to being strikes. So I sent one of my guys up to the plate without a bat. The umpire made him come back and get one. But I made my point, swing at good pitches. It was a teaching tool and I made it fun.

Another thing I've learned is to never underestimate the psychological aspect of the game. Players have to have the right mindset to win. That's something I learned in 1973 when I first managed in the majors with the Royals. Bill Harrison, who is still a good friend of mine, had this thing he called vision training, where you visualized your success. He was on the cutting edge of that stuff. His company today is called Performance Fundamentals. He taught me some important things. Players can't be worried about too much. They need to focus on the game, on each pitch and nothing else.

One time when I was managing in Omaha, the GM, Bob Quinn, decided to have the players ride in a parade on the Fourth of July after they had just returned from a long road trip. I said we were going to lose the next two games because of that parade—the players were focusing on being mad about having to do the parade and not on winning. Unfortunately, I was right. That's exactly what happened.

Another time, Bill Beck (who has been the Marlins' director of team travel for the last 14 years, and who was our traveling secretary and play-by-play broadcaster at Omaha in 1969, and who later worked with me in San Diego), decided to pay the players before the game. Some guy sees $1.35 taken out of his paycheck for something or other and he starts moaning, "What's going on here?" I told Bill, "We'll lose tonight. Don't ever pay anyone before the game." We lost and Bill never paid anyone right before a game again.

Same thing happens with today's ballplayers. If they are upset over something, they won't play right. Don't burden ballplayers with the unexpected, don't disrupt their program.

My philosophy with players has always been tough love. You've got to discipline them. They appreciate the discipline. That's lost today in a lot of ways.

What I tried to make the Marlins realize from the first day I arrived was how good they could be. God had given them so much talent they were not taking advantage of because they were not working as hard as they could have been. Some of these guys come into the big leagues so used to being babied that they don't know how to get the most out of their ability. They don't know how to push themselves.

But I do. I may be 74 years old, but I'm always looking to win another World Series. I like challenges. That's what life is all about.

It's funny, at the All-Star Game this past year, Tal Smith, who is with the Astros front office, said to me, "Jack, you've ruined it for everybody. You started a trend, taking over sputtering clubs, you've done it three or four times now." Then he smiled and said, "Too bad you're not available."

I wasn't, but Phil Garner was. He replaced Jimy Williams and did a great job with that team. He gave them new life as the Astros won the wild-card, just like we did the year before. I guess I *was* a trendsetter.

I think the Marlins can be a contender for years. The great thing is that Jeffrey Loria always wants to get better, and he runs a great organization with the team's president, David Samson. GM Larry Beinfest has made terrific deals to energize the team.

It's important to remember a team and players become popular when you win—there's no other reason. Winning makes you popular. Sometimes you have to make the hard decisions and trade the popular guy for a chance to win. I traded Hall of Fame shortstop Ozzie Smith in San Diego when I was GM after the 1981 season. There was no more popular guy in a city than Ozzie Smith was in San Diego. I didn't trade him because of that, but because he demanded so much money from ownership. What I got in return was an All-Star shortstop in Garry Templeton. I got right-fielder Sixto Lezcano and relief pitcher Luis DeLeon, both of whom made our club better. We made it to the World Series two years later. It wasn't a popular decision at the time, but nobody was complaining when we went to the World Series. And when we went, I lit up a victory cigar.

Some GMs don't understand that, they think it is impossible to trade a popular player. Don't go sideways or backwards, go forward. Don't be afraid to make the bold move. Be creative.

I'm always thinking, especially when I'm taking my walk and smoking my cigar.

CHAPTER 3

Seasoned Citizens

I've been around so long I remember when Preparation H was Preparation A.

Some people see me as the poster child for senior citizens. I don't look at us as senior citizens, we're *seasoned citizens*. When I was named manager of the Marlins, I used the term *seasoned citizen* in my first press conference. I thanked Jeffrey Loria for taking a chance on a seasoned citizen.

A lot of the so-called experts thought I was too old for this job, guys like Rob Dibble. A guy in Atlanta wrote that I would have to skip Tuesday games so it wouldn't conflict with bingo night at the senior citizen home. Bingo! I got myself in the record books. I became one of only two managers to lead my team to a World Series title after taking over in midseason. Bob Lemon was the other manager who did that when he took over the Yankees for Billy Martin in 1978. Funny how it goes, I took over for Bob Lemon in Kansas City in 1973.

I won some awards, too. I was named the 2003 Sportsman of the Year by *The Sporting News* along with Dick Vermeil, coach of the Chiefs. Dick's only a kid, he was 67. I was nearly 73. I also won my second Manager of the Year award in five years, given by the Baseball Writers Association of America. I was the first manager hired during the season to ever win the award and the oldest manager to win it.

I also was the oldest manager to reach the postseason for the first time and the oldest manager to reach the World Series. And, of course, I was the oldest manager to win a World Series.

After we won it all, my son Kasey said, "There aren't many people who can say they've done just about everything in baseball, including winning the World Series. And seeing how much this business can age you in a hurry, my dad's aged pretty well." That's because I love to get out there and get involved with people. That's the way I approach life. I always try to have fun. My message to other seasoned citizens is this: go out and live your life. Enjoy it. Go out and volunteer. Look at me bouncing around. Join church groups. Get involved with youth groups and charitable organizations. I've stayed young because I'm around young people. Don't sit in a rocking chair and rot away. You've got time left. Go out and enjoy it.

It's not how old you are that's important. It's how old you act. I manage to live because I live to manage. This past year, I was named one of the 10 most influential senior citizens, along with General Tommy Franks and actress Jessica Lange, by AARP. That's pretty good company.

I don't act my age. My birth certificate says I'm 74, but I don't feel 74. I've never felt old. When people ask me how old I feel—and they always ask me that—I say I feel like I'm 45. I can't believe I'm 74. After we beat the Giants in the Division Series and went to play the Cubs, I said I felt like I was 38. After we beat the Cubs and went to the

World Series, I felt like I was 28, and after we beat the Yankees to win the whole thing, I felt like I was 18.

Jeffrey Loria had the guts to hire an old goat like me, and then re-hire me and re-hire me again. He put it best, telling a reporter, "I couldn't care if Jack was 78 or 85, as long as he presents himself the way he does: his intensity, his knowledge, his energy."

There is a group in Miami called Ascending Life, which pushes for seasoned citizens to get involved in different activities. The archdiocesan director is Hugh Clear, who is my age. He says the motto of the group is "Live while you live."

I like that. He said I'm not a youth, but I am youthful. I like that too. Back in Alamance County in North Carolina where I live, I love to help out in food drives and other charitable events. I get a kick out of whatever I'm doing. Put your talents to good use. And if you don't like something, don't be afraid to speak up. You've earned the right to say what you think.

I'm not afraid to speak up. We were in Montreal for the last major league game ever played there and the fans were booing the hell out of the United States National Anthem. They booed the heck out of the singer. It was an embarrassment and a disgrace. It wasn't right, so I said something. The fans didn't like that either.

Oh, well, that's history. There's no more Major League Baseball in Montreal. We don't have to worry about that anymore. It's not the first ballpark I've closed, although it's the first time I shut down baseball in another country.

When Met fans were booing their old closer Armando Benitez when we were in New York during the 2004 season, I told the reporters to make sure to tell the fans, "Come on out and boo him tomorrow, too." Hey, you've gotta have fun.

The first day of spring training in 2004, I felt like a kid again. They found someone 27 years older than me to throw out the first ball in Jupiter, Florida, where we train. I was the catcher and she threw the ball. Her name was Maude Newkirk and she just turned 100. She had a great time. She was wearing a Dontrelle Willis jersey and she caught me by surprise. She threw the ball overhand. I was expecting her to throw underhand. After she made the throw, I told her she could have moved back another 10 feet and thrown a strike.

I'm always looking out for the seasoned citizen. After we won the World Series, we were invited to Tallahassee to speak to all the politicians. On the floor of the Florida House of Representatives I said, "I'm here representing the senior citizens of Florida. I want to propose a couple of bills. The first one is that we repeal the anti-smoking law. I think there should be an amendment to it so that any senior citizen over 65 can smoke anywhere in the state."

The place broke up.

"The next thing I want to propose," and I didn't know they were actually talking about it for two days, "is that we do something about the state fuel tax. We ought to reduce the tax to help the senior citizens. They're on a fixed income, they can't afford this." So, afterward, all these senators came down and started congratulating me, two representatives even said, "Hey, you really helped us out with that fuel comment."

A little while later I was sitting outside the building smoking my last cigar. Larry Beinfest and I decided to walk down the street to see if we could find any more cigars. Who do we run into but a lobbyist for the Cigar Association for America? I said to him, "You're just the guy I want." Five minutes later he was handing us some great cigars. That's the story of my life. I'm always getting breaks like that. That's why I say over and over, I've been blessed. The Good Lord is always looking out for me.

There's a 50-year age difference between me and a lot of players, but I find a way to get along with them. I remember when second baseman Luis Castillo came up to me and put his arm around me and asked, "How come you are so nice?"

"Cause I love you guys," I told him.

He said, "That's why we play hard for you, Jack."

The young guys have always been the greatest to deal with. When I was in Cincinnati managing players like Sean Casey and Pokey Reese, they were a pleasure to work with. Every time I see them, they come over and give me a big hug.

I've been around great ballplayers since 1947. That's when Allie Clark was playing with the Newark Bears. Every night I'd go up to Bears Stadium with him and I'd catch batting practice and work out with him. That's when Yogi Berra was there and Bobby Brown, some great players.

My managing mentor was Danny Murtaugh. He managed the Pirates for 15 years. He was one of the best ever. Danny was beautiful. I was in spring training with him in 1953, and he was a great double-talker. He had a sidekick, Bill Burrell, who was his pitching coach. I was a young kid getting a chance to go to spring training with a Double-A club down in New Orleans, and I was excited. We were playing the Cardinals. I was sitting in the middle of the bench, and I didn't know Danny was a great double-talker. He had a big chew of tobacco in his mouth—you didn't dare walk by him because if you did he would spray your pants with tobacco juice and get a big laugh out of it.

He looked down the bench and said, "Hey Mac, why don't you . . ." then it was nothing but double-talking gibberish. The only word I heard after that was "bullpen."

So I said, "What Danny? You want me to go down to the bullpen?"

"No, no, that's all right," he said. He was joking with me and I didn't know it.

Then a few minutes later he did it to me again, and the only words I could get were *balls* and *bullpen*.

I said, "What, Danny? You want me to take some balls down to the bullpen?"

He's got me jumping up and down and finally I realized he's busting my chops. He did that to everybody, it was fun. That's where I learned early on, from a great manager, that this game is supposed to be fun.

When I was in the minors we used to sit around in the lobby with the old-time managers and talk all the time. Wes Griffin was the manager I had at Hutchinson, Kansas. I laugh now because we considered this guy an old-timer. He was only 60. He was just a kid. But he was a crusty old guy who played with Ty Cobb and he'd tell us about Cobb, how in between innings, "We'd sharpen his spikes."

Wes taught all the young pitchers how to throw the spitball. We'd sit around the clubhouse or the hotel lobby and get so much knowledge about the game. He'd educate us. Today you don't do that because everybody wants to get the heck out of the clubhouse so quickly after a game.

Wes was a big hunter so we all chipped in and brought him a shotgun for his birthday. One night in a game we had some college-educated guy on third base. We're down 4–1, and he tells Wes Griffith, "Skip, I can steal home." Now you don't go stealing home when you're down, 4–1.

Wes says, "Son, you go right ahead. Because when you start out, I'm going for the shotgun. We'll see who gets there first."

The college kid never did steal home.

I have fun in all parts of the game. I had some fun with that little biography that appears in the press guides. A couple years ago a writer from New York called me out of the blue. I was sitting at home in North Carolina in one of my retirement phases.

The writer said that Barry Zito, the pitcher for the A's during that year's playoffs, said classical music kind of relaxed him, and then the reporter asked me, "What does it do for you, Jack?"

I started laughing and said, "What do you mean?"

"You know, classical music. Zito says it makes him relax, what's it do for you?"

"I don't know a damn thing about classical music," I said.

"That's funny," he said. "I went through 150 biographies, and you were the only guy that I saw in there where it had hobbies, you put down classical music and opera."

I started laughing again. I told him I just got tired of reading the same old stuff about ballplayers' favorite hobbies. It's always the same thing—hunting, fishing, and golf—so I decided to do something different. I put down opera and classical music. I don't know a thing about opera and classical music.

I do like classical music, though—classical stuff like Frank Sinatra and Perry Como. One day Bill Beck was telling me about how he and his wife, Vesna, took in the opera and some Broadway plays while on a trip to New York. About three weeks later I called him in Florida. While the phone was ringing, a light flashed on in my head, and when Vesna answered, I told her I was from a ticket company in New York and I had her tickets for the concert, featuring the famous violinist, Skolivinak (I just made up a name).

Vesna hemmed and hawed and told me she didn't order any tickets, and I argued that we had her order. She was getting upset, and I sensed she was ready to hang up on me. "Wait a minute," I said, starting to laugh, "this is Jack McKeon."

"I guess you got me this time," she said.

Another time she asked me what composers I liked. Before I answered, I went down to the local liquor store and wrote down some names. I told her, "Smirnoff's a hell of a composer, isn't he?"

This past year I got the chance to go to the ESPYs. I had to be the oldest guy there, but I had fun. The Marlins got beat for Coach of the Year and Team of the Year by Larry Brown and the Pistons—I think it was more of a basketball crowd than a baseball crowd—but Carol and I still had a great time, and it was good to see another old guy like Larry win. I was one of only five people in the place with a tux on. These kinds of affairs used to all be tux affairs, now they call it fashionable chic. You know what fashionable chic is? Put on a white shirt and let it hang out to your butt and throw a coat on top of it, that's fashionable chic.

That was the same week I got the chance to manage the National League All-Star team. It was great to be in the clubhouse with so many future Hall of Famers and so many class-act guys. When you looked at the make-up of the All-Star team you saw a bunch of winners. I wished I could have brought a couple of them back with me to Florida.

Being around a guy like Roger Clemens was terrific, he's such an ambassador for the game. And I hooked him up with Mike Piazza. They got together in a brief meeting. They had had some problems in the past—Roger hit Mike in the head a few years ago. I thought bringing them together might be good for closure for both of them. The media wanted to make a big issue out of it, but these two guys are very professional, and they went about their meeting in a very professional way.

I talked with Mike about the situation. I asked him what he thought if I decided to start Clemens and if he would catch him.

"Are you going to have any problem with that?" I asked.

Mike was great, he said, "No, Jack. I just appreciate the opportunity. I'm glad you talked to me about it. I'm not going to have a problem, and I'm sure Roger won't either. Both of us are professionals. I can handle that situation, don't worry about it, but it was nice that you asked me about it."

The guy I felt bad for in Houston was Astros manager Jimy Williams, who got booed by his hometown fans and was about to be fired. Believe me, I know all about being fired. I didn't think that was very Houston-like, the way they treated Jimy. I didn't think that was very courteous.

As for the game, just watching the American League team was something. I was sitting over in my dugout, drooling with what Joe Torre had to put out there every day with his lineup: Gary Sheffield, Alex Rodriguez, Derek Jeter, Jason Giambi, Bernie Williams.

Because we had played the Mets in Florida right before the All-Star Game, we went over to Houston and took the Mets who were going to the game with us, guys like Tom Glavine, Piazza, and some Mets officials.

I got to visit with Glavine, his wife, and his kids—Tommy is another class-act guy, and he has a really nice family. So just before the game, I was sitting down there talking to Danny Graves from Cincinnati, and Glavine's little boy, a great kid, came up to me and said, "Skip, who's starting tonight?"

"Well, who do you want to start?" I said.

"Randy Johnson or Tom," he said.

I just laughed. I could have gone with Randy or Tommy, but I thought the night belonged to Roger Clemens. I went with the seasoned citizen. If I hadn't started Roger, those fans in Houston never would have let me get out of there alive.

The great thing about going to the World Series and the All-Star Game was that it brought so much attention to my age. Somebody said I'm a cult figure to the 70-and-over set. That's fine with me. I feel that the Good Lord put me in this position to help invigorate other seasoned citizens.

Larry Beinfest said it best in an article he wrote for the *Rocky Mountain News*. "Nothing gets by Jack," he wrote. "He's with it. He has the ability to adjust. It doesn't matter whether you're 20 or 40 or 60—Jack's 33 years older than me—he's a people person, and he knows how to do it.

"His experience was valuable, but his ability to adjust to different personalities and figure out the right way to get the most out of players is, I think, one of his true talents.

"What you see is what you get with Jack. Jack's his own man. He's not a politician. His agenda was to turn around this team and to win. And that's what he did and he did it his way."

Just like Frank Sinatra.

I like the way David Samson put it, too. He said, "Jack lulls you into a false sense of foolishness, and he wraps that around a level of intelligence, from a baseball standpoint, that is incredible."

None of this would have been said if I just stayed home and watched TV. So get up out of that rocking chair and make something happen. Get a job. Live your life to the fullest. I have.

Maybe I'll even see you next year at the ESPYs.

CHAPTER 4

Always the Showman

Here are some of my tested principles for both baseball and, of course, life:

- Enjoy each game; enjoy each moment, each pitch, nothing is promised.
- You are never too old to become older, and never too old to become younger.
- Draw lessons from the past, don't live in the past.
- Steer clear of too much self-examination. You don't want the small stuff to make you sweat.
- Speak plainly and carry a big stogie.
- If effort lags, light 'em up. Players need and want discipline.
- Mix and match, play your hunches.
- Failure isn't fatal.
- Have a role for your role players.

- When a player falls, never keep him down. Help him up.
- Check your ego at the door. Praise your players and coaches, they are the ones who got you there.
- Seize the moment.
- The Good Lord has a plan for you.
- Baseball is entertainment.
- Always pack an extra box of cigars.
- Get to the ballpark early.
- Never complain when your wife goes shopping.

Those are my rules to live by, and I have done just that, for the most part. Take the one about baseball being entertainment. When you're in the minor leagues as long as I was, you never forget that. When I was managing in the minors, we'd go to a town, and the opposing general manager would corner me and say, "Jack, how can you help us get the crowd up?"

"What do you want me to do?"

"Do something crazy."

They came to the right guy.

We were playing in Great Falls, Montana, one night in 1956. I was a 25-year-old player/manager. This GM asked me to do something to jump up the crowd. In the old days in the minor leagues, you generally had a light pole just a little bit behind first base in foul territory, nothing like the poles of today. These were just wooden telephone poles.

So I went out there early before the game to check out the pole. I stuck my spikes in it, but the rung was far above my head. I'm listed at 5'10", but that might not be the truth, so that rung was pretty far up there. I knew I could jump and reach the rung, so I figured I'd do something special for the crowd.

That night, I got up with two outs in the inning. I hit a ground ball to third base and they threw me out, but I just kept on running hard toward that telephone pole, about 20 feet behind first. I threw my spikes into the wood, grabbed hold of the rung, swung myself up, and climbed halfway up the pole.

The people were going crazy, yelling, "Put him in a cage!"

The next day the fans brought me all kinds of stuff, including the type of tobacco I used to chew. I did what the guy wanted. I jumped up the crowd.

At times, my players would get carried away with their practical jokes. In 1960, in Wilson, North Carolina, I had this lefty pitcher named Don Koudis. Lefties generally are known as being a little crazy. Well, Koudis was worse than that. He used to room with the bus driver, "Peg Leg" Bates. At night, Peg Leg would take off his wooden leg and stick it by his bed. One night, Koudis thought it would be funny to hide Peg Leg's peg leg. The next morning I got a frantic call from Peg Leg. Koudis was gone and so was the peg leg. I rushed to Bates' room and luckily I found his leg hidden on the top shelf of the closet.

Sometimes I would combine my scouting and entertaining side. I'm always looking for players to improve the team, and I'm not afraid to have fun while I'm doing it. I'll go anywhere to look at a player, even the zoo. In 1969 when I was managing Triple A Omaha, I cooked something up with sportscaster Dave Blackwell.

The team was in first place and Dave wanted to do something to spice up his report. I knew they had this orangutan at the zoo named Casey, and, with the approval of the zookeeper, we played some ball with Casey. We went to his cage, threw him a baseball, and he bit it and started pounding his chest, just like in the movies. Then he started throwing the ball against the wall. We decided to have more fun and give Casey a bat. What's better than Casey at the Bat. All this time Dave had his cameraman filming the action. Casey was a natural. He picked up the bat and put it on his shoulder, just like a real ballplayer. It looked like he was posing for a baseball card. He eventually took a bite of the bat, too.

The cameraman then shot me standing on the other side of the cage with a contract and an Omaha cap in my hands to make it look like I was there ready to sign Casey. So that night, before the game Dave asked me on camera. "Jack, you're only four games in front. Do you need to make a move for pennant insurance?"

"Well, Dave," I said. "I got a guy who is about 6'5" and nearly 500 pounds. He swings a mean bat and he's got some arm. And as you know, we're always looking to get better. The only problem is his temper."

Dave then asked, "Can we take a look at him, Jack?"

I said, "Sure, Dave," and with that they rolled the film from the zoo. Like I always say, this game is supposed to be fun.

I like to have fun, but my teams always are serious when it comes to winning games. My son-in-law, Greg Booker, pitched for the Padres until I traded him. I think he said it best: he said I bring a fun mood to the clubhouse. Then he added, "But don't dare discount his knowledge about the game. If it was all about just having fun and making the clubhouse lighter, teams would hire Jay Leno to manage. That's not the case. No one knows the game better than Jack. He does not miss a thing."

Now you know why my daughter Kristi married him.

In my earlier years in the minors, I had to kid around a lot because it was a way to draw crowds to the game and that was part of the business. I guess I'm a little bit like Bill Veeck, the great owner and showman, who used to own the Indians and once sent a midget up to hit.

I've always had fun around the game, even when I was a kid and even when I was in the air force. My friends still kid me about my sharpshooting medal. I coached the baseball team at Samson Air Force base. One of my pitchers was a military policeman. When I had to go qualify for shooting the rifle on the next Tuesday, I made sure my buddy the MP went. A couple days later, I was on the list as a sharpshooter.

People who have listened to me talk know I'm a sharpshooter in some ways. And I've been sharpshooting for a long time when it comes to talking about baseball. I just have a feel about this game. After the All-Star break in the 2003 season, I had a feeling about the Marlins and I told the writers that we could win the wild-card. At the time I said, "I know it's a tall order, but I believe in miracles. This club really hasn't been on a long, eight-game winning streak, but you've got to shoot for the moon."

That's what I mean by being a sharpshooter. A friend of mine sent me a story from when I first started managing in the major leagues with the Royals in 1973. It's funny, I still have many of the same ideas, they're just a little more refined. Years ago I said, "Our whole theme is going to be 'How to win.' I want the Royals to be known as the smartest team in baseball." We had won 8 of our first 10 games, and I said:

> I wanted to modernize the thinking of the ballplayer. I go along with the modern day thinking. Times have changed. We drive 1973 cars now instead of 1930 Model A's, and we have a breed of players entirely different from those of 1949 when I started playing.
>
> I think it's a good breed. I try to treat my players like men by recognizing their individuality and their philosophy. You're

concerned with their entire lives, not just whether they hit .300 or win 20 games.

I may not make better players out of all of them, but I'll make better men out of them.

I understand it all better now. Players have changed since 1973, and it's time to change with the times again. In 2005, we're not driving the same cars we drove in 1973.

Some things haven't changed, like throwing strikes. The pitcher has to get ahead of the hitter. There was this game in San Diego, soon after I took over the Marlins. Dontrelle Willis was on the mound. We were losing, 3–0, and then went ahead, 7–3, and he goes back out there and walks the first batter he sees. Then he falls behind 2–0 on the next guy. I ran out there and let him have it. I got right in his face and screamed, "What the [bleep] are you doing? Throw a strike!"

The kid was only 21 and he probably never heard it exactly in those terms before, but he did what I told him to do, and we got out of the inning with no problems. He got his first win that day.

You have to play hurt, too, in this game. I was catching in Pittsfield, Massachusetts, when Brooks Lawrence, who went on to pitch with the Reds, took this big swing and hit this little dribbler right in front of the plate. For a fat kid, I moved pretty fast, and I was all over this ball. I was too quick. Lawrence's backswing smacked right into my forehead. There was blood everywhere. They told me that women passed out in the stands. I was taken to the hospital and stitched up. The doctors wanted to keep me for observation, but they didn't observe me sneaking out of the hospital that night. I was back with the team the next morning. A few days later I was pitching batting practice and accidentally hit our backup catcher in the leg with a pitch. He couldn't catch after that hit.

I was ready. I said, "I'm fine, Skip, I can catch." Wouldn't you know it, the very first inning a foul tip catches me right on the mask in the forehead, and a couple stitches pop open. The blood came pouring out again, but I just had the trainer slap a big bandage on my forehead. A few innings later I took another shot to the mask, same area, more blood, more stitches pop open.

We had a doubleheader that day, and in the second game, one of their batters got in an argument with the umpire, dropped his bat, and hit me right in the head. Now six of the eight stitches were open and there was blood all around home plate. The umpire was getting sick to his stomach, I was bleeding all over the balls, but I stayed in there. Like I say, you gotta play hurt.

And you have to make people feel wanted in this game. That's one of the secrets. You have to make your players feel good, you have to make your fans feel good, and you need to please your advertisers, too. There are all kinds of little ways you can do that. In San Diego I attended many charity dinners where everything was black tie, so I got myself a deal with Brady's Men's Shop. Jerry Coleman, our announcer, had a deal with the guy, too, and every time I went on the air I was asked by Jerry, "What did you do today?" and I'd say, "Well, I went down to Brady's Men's Shop." I'd get all the stuff for free. Then when I'd be speaking at a function, I'd have somebody near me hand me a note and I'd say, throwing anybody's name in there, "Mr. Harboy, I got a note here from Brady's Men's Shop, get that sport coat back by 10:00." That would break up the place. I'd get a laugh and I'd get Brady's a plug.

The best one was when I helped marketing whiz John Shean get the Padres a $5-million deal with Toyota. I did a commercial with them, too. In that commercial I wore a Padres uniform. The ad campaign ran the first year and was a huge success and everyone was happy. The second year of the deal, one of the Padres bean counters told me, "Jack, we want $10,000 to let you use our uniform in the commercial." I was determined to teach them a lesson, so I called Rawlings and said, "I want you to make me a shirt, identical to the Padres uniform. Instead of Padres across the chest, I want 'Trader Jack' across the chest." They did just that. I didn't wear a Padres uniform for the commercials. I wore a "Trader Jack" jersey.

The Padres bean counter saw it and said, "What is he doing wearing a Trader Jack shirt?" The account executive working the ad said, "Well, you wouldn't let him wear a Padres uniform."

I fixed them!

All that, though, is off-the-field stuff. On the field you have to concentrate in this game and at the same time be loose. You have to pay attention to what's happening on the field. This goes for everyone. I want the players who aren't playing to be watching the game on the bench and getting into the game.

That's why when I took over with the Marlins I knew some guys were watching the first few innings of the game in the clubhouse—relaxing on recliners in the air-conditioned clubhouse. The heck with that. I made sure they sat with the rest of us in the heat by locking the clubhouse door. That got their attention and they were soon out there watching with the rest of us. The only way to win in this game is as a team.

That's the secret to this game. Have fun, but know what you're doing. Winning is fun. It's like the time I was in the minors and we were playing in Denver. We were the visiting team and I just got tired of the home team shooting off fireworks after one of their guys hit a home run.

So I got myself a gun that shot blanks, and when one of our guys hit a home run, I pulled out my pistol and went, Pow! Pow! The guys got a big kick out of that. It made everybody loose and we played better. We hit more home runs and I got more chances to shoot that pistol.

Remember, I am a sharpshooter.

CHAPTER 5

Branching Out

The book *Moneyball* is the rage in baseball these days. But I don't use that line of thinking as much as some people do. Moneyball is basically computer stats. I think my style is more observation and going with your gut.

I never learned my baseball out of a book. I learned it by doing it and watching the best in the game do it. I go all the way back to Branch Rickey, who signed Jackie Robinson to play for the Dodgers.

Some of the stuff in *Moneyball* has merit, there's no question about it. But you can't just go by numbers. How far back do the numbers go? Has the player changed? It doesn't take into consideration the mental approach he has today or the mental state he is in today. What if his kid's in the hospital? Maybe he is not as focused as he normally is because of that.

Branch Rickey was a highly intelligent guy and was very creative. I was signed as a catcher in 1949 by the Pirates. A year later Rickey was the man in charge of the Pirates. He was the guy who came up with the idea of "farming out" talent to nurture it. He was the guy who enabled

African Americans to play in the majors. He was a baseball genius, and he changed the game in a great way.

He also was a guy in a business suit working his magic with players. Today they would probably ridicule him.

I used to marvel at his teaching tools. When he was trying to teach a guy to throw a curveball down low and just off the plate, he would lay a $20 bill right there on the ground. He'd say, "If you hit the $20 bill, you got it."

Now to me, that's "moneyball." That got the pitchers focused. They had to follow through and come down through their motion. It was a great incentive. It was not only a fun thing, it was a teaching tool. I've never forgotten that.

That same drill would work today, but you would have to use a $100 bill.

Rickey also was one of the first guys to put up strings for the strike zone as a teaching tool, which I copied and used to teach Jim Kaat when I had him in the minors. Rickey would get two poles, put strings across them, and make it the size of the strike zone. He would have the guys hit the inside corner, the outside corner, up and down, all around the plate. It was a great way to teach location. Rickey didn't know it at the time, but he developed the first K Zone.

Rickey also was one tough negotiator.

When I signed in 1949, I was paid $215 a month. In 1952 I had made it all the way to $225 a month; the next year they signed me for $237.50. I went to spring training with New Orleans. After spring training, they moved me from Class C to Class B, and we went into the office one by one to meet with Mr. Rickey.

He was sitting there behind this great big desk and said, "Here's your contract. It's for $250."

"I want $275."

He said, "It's either $250 or there is the door."

"Mr. Rickey, give me the pen."

The man knew his numbers. Today you've got so many statistics in the game, people don't even know what they're looking at. There was a game in 2003 against Tommy Glavine. The writers asked me if I was going to catch Mike Redmond against Glavine instead of Pudge Rodriguez. I said, "No. Why?"

"Well Redmond hits Glavine good," they told me. "He hits .485 against Glavine."

I said, "I don't give a damn. I'm going to catch the best guy I've got." So what happened? Pudge hit a home run and won the game.

Statistics have some value. I tell the story about Tony Solaita. I was managing the Royals and we were playing Detroit. John Mayberry, who was my first baseman, was hurt. Before the game, the trainer came to me and said, "Hey, Solaita can't see. He's got an infection in his eye. It's swollen. One eye is closed."

I was going to take him out of the lineup, so I said, "Tony, I don't want to take the chance of your getting hurt because you can't see."

He said, "Skip, it's OK. I can hit this guy with one eye. Every time I face him, I hit one out of the park."

First time up, two men on—bingo. He hit one on top of the roof at Tiger Stadium. With one eye.

One of the greatest things about my career has been getting the chance to work for so many different owners who were from so many different backgrounds.

People sometimes looked at me as being cocky, abrasive. But if I worked for you, I always told you the truth. A lot of times, people don't want to hear the truth. You get a lot of jealousy involved with executives who sometimes tell ownership what they think they want to hear. I'm not afraid to tell it the way I see it. I'm very secure in giving my opinion and being held responsible.

You encounter that jealousy especially after you win. Tal Smith was a consultant with the Padres in 1984 after we won the pennant, and I was GM. He told me that it was going to be different from then on, and he was right.

He said, "Jack, when you win, everybody wants to take credit for winning and everyone is shooting at you."

I've worked for everyone from Marge Schott to Ted Turner, and I've always had the same philosophy. Don't be afraid to put your neck on the line. Sooner or later in this game, even if you don't put your neck on the line, it's going to get chopped off, anyway. So at least have the satisfaction of not being a yes man.

I managed Triple A Richmond for the Braves in the International League in 1976. Ted Turner came over Opening Day to see us play, and Johnny Sain was my pitching coach, so we all went out to dinner. The Atlanta Braves had started off real good, winning seven out of ten, and he was raving about the club. I told him, "Ted, your club is not that good."

I could have kept quiet and said he had a good club, but I knew they were going to struggle. I had to tell him the truth. I told him, "Your club has too many holes."

"No, they're going to be great," he shot back.

"No Ted, some of those guys you've got, they can't play."

So the season went on, and we made the playoffs. The Braves were finishing up a 70–92 season in last place. We played Rochester in the playoffs, and Ted came in to see us. We went out to dinner again, and he banged his fist on the table and said, "Jack, you were right. You told me right from the start we were no good."

Ted took a liking to me after that, and he wanted me to come over and work with him. I told him I would rather stay and manage Richmond. About a week later, Charlie Finley, the owner of the Oakland A's, called. I was managing in Puerto Rico then in the Winter League, so on my way back to Chicago to see Charlie, I had to stop in Atlanta. I called Ted and said, "Ted, I don't have to worry about making a decision, I just decided to take the A's job."

He said, "You're crazy, you know you're going to get fired."

"I know that."

"Jack, you always have a job with me. Call me after you get fired."

I never did call him, but I always had that ace in the hole because I told him the truth instead of doing what most guys do—tell the owner what they want to hear.

Charlie Finley did eventually fire me, and rehire me, and fire me. But we had a lot of fun together. He had some crazy ideas. He'd get up and say: "We've got lousy pitching, we've got lousy hitting, but we're going to steal the pennant."

We had four or five rabbits—guys who could really run. We didn't have any players, but we had guys who could run. One day he was talking to me in a team meeting and said, "If you don't watch out, before you know it, the Indians will be coming over the wall."

So we finished the meeting, the game started, and about the sixth inning the phone rang in the dugout. It was the bullpen, and the voice on the other end said, "Hey, skip, the Indians are coming over the wall. Get ready!"

One year in spring training, I had made a deal for Ron Guidry from the Yankees, and Charlie told me, "What do you know about Guidry?" So Charlie killed the deal. The season started, and Guidry threw a two-hit shutout against us in Oakland. He was throwing another shutout against us in Yankee Stadium on national television on Monday night. We were behind 4–0 going into the eighth inning. The phone rang in the dugout. I picked it up. It was Charlie in Chicago. "Tell those guys to choke up," he ordered.

"They are, Charlie."

He said, "I'm watching the game, they're not choking up."

Miguel Dilone was my leadoff hitter. I was going to have him take a strike anyway, so I said, "Come here. Give me that bat."

I showed him how I wanted him to choke up three quarters of the way up the bat, past the label. I sent him up there and said, "Now that SOB in Chicago is not going to tell me these guys aren't choking up."

Dilone didn't get a hit, but Charlie didn't call again that night. He saw his batters choking up.

Every night, if we weren't hitting, Charlie would call to tell me to tell them to choke up. It got so, as soon as I hung up the phone in the dugout, guys on the bench would start hollering, "Choke up. Choke up."

One night we were playing the Royals. It was the top of the eighth and we were behind 2–1. We had the bases loaded, nobody out. Whitey Herzog was managing the Royals and brought in Al Hrabosky, "the Mad Hungarian." While they were making the pitching change, the phone rang.

It was Charlie. He said slowly, "Consider the squeeze."

"OK, Charlie."

There was no way I was going to squeeze in the eighth inning with the bases loaded and nobody out. Jeff Newman was the first hitter. He got ahead 2–0 on the count and then swung and missed three straight pitches. Joe Wallis was the next hitter—two balls and no strikes. I knew Hrabosky would walk the park if they didn't swing. But Wallis swung at three straight pitches out of the strike zone and struck out. Pee Wee Edwards came up, a little second baseman. He swung at the first pitch, pop fly to second base. Before the guy caught the ball, the phone rang again.

It was Charlie. "You dumb SOB. I told you to squeeze."

When Charlie got really mad at you, he wouldn't call. So that was good. Another day we were in Cleveland, and Dock Ellis, the next day's pitcher, took the pitching chart into the shower, put a match to it, and burned it up. Dock didn't believe in pitching charts.

Well, at the time, I didn't know any of this happened. Charlie found out about it from one of his clubhouse spies. The next day I got a call about 6:00 in the morning.

"Say, Jack, do we kind of keep any charts on the pitchers? Do we have the chart from last night?"

"Yeah, Charlie, Lee Stange, the pitching coach, has it."

"What room is Stange in?"

He called Stange. "Do we have last night's pitching chart?"

Stange told him, "No, Dock Ellis burned it last night in the shower."

"Does Jack know about this?"

Stange said, "No, I haven't told him yet."

So that time I got off the hook. But to be honest, that pitching chart stuff can be a bunch of garbage, too. Half the time the guy keeping the chart isn't paying attention and asks the guy next to him, "Hey, what was that pitch?"

When Charlie signed slugger Dick Allen, who was nearing the end of his career, he called me to pick Allen up at the airport in Phoenix. We had no public relations director—I was the manager and the public relations director. So I got this press conference together, went and picked up Dick Allen, who was a difficult player to get along with, and introduced him. He got up and said, "I'm a changed man. I'm a born-again Christian."

Some writer asked him, "What is your role?"

"Whatever the manager wants me to do," Dick said.

I thought to myself, "That's good."

We started the season; we opened up with the Twins. We played him on a Saturday and we won. Sunday we had a doubleheader. I played him the first game. Thinking I was giving him a breather, the second game I started him at designated hitter. The first inning Dick said to me, "I ain't DH-ing. I got it in my deal with Charlie, I don't DH."

So I had to pinch-hit in the first inning for the DH. So much for being a changed man.

I thought we could get a great year out of Dick if we could give him a day off once a week. I called Charlie and he said, "No way. I'm paying him to play every day."

Dick would call Charlie and ask for a day off sometimes, and Charlie would tell him, "It's not up to me, it's up to my manager. I don't interfere with my manager."

Right after Dick called Charlie to tell him he needed a day off, Charlie sent him a case of Geritol. Charlie always had someone working the phones for him, spying and letting him know what was going on every day on the field and in the clubhouse.

One of his spies really knew how to rap, a young kid Charlie nick-named Hammer because he reminded him of Hank Aaron. Years later the young man was known as MC Hammer.

I got along well with Hammer. I had to. Charlie had made him a vice president at the age of 16.

Hammer used to sit up in the press box and broadcast the games on the phone back to Charlie in Chicago. The kid was a natural. Hammer would call Charlie back in Chicago and give him play-by-play— remember this was before you could watch all the games on TV.

The kid knew exactly what Charlie wanted. Even then, Hammer knew how to play to the crowd. When one of Charlie's rabbits was on first base and wouldn't steal, Hammer would yell into the phone, "Charlie, he didn't go! He didn't go!"

That would just make Charlie more upset: "Hammer, why didn't he go?"

"I don't know, Charlie, I don't know. Jack must be holding back the rabbit."

I was getting second-guessed on every pitch. If the pitcher was struggling and there was no one warming up in the bullpen, Hammer would yell into the phone: "Charlie, nobody's warming up!"

One time we were winning 9–0 and Joe Coleman started losing it. Charlie wanted to know why somebody wasn't warming up.

After I got fired, and I was working as an assistant GM for Charlie because I was still under contract, I was up in the press box sitting next to Hammer. Hammer had to run back to the office to get something for Charlie, so he handed the phone to me. It was my turn to be a broadcaster.

I wasn't very good at it. I gave Charlie the count, "It's 3–1, Charlie." Then I'd pause for about 10 seconds and give an update, "Grounder to short. He's out."

Charlie got angry. "Jack, you've got to learn how to broadcast, you've got to do it like Hammer does it. You've got to say things like: 'The pitcher's in the stretch, the runner at first takes a short lead, he checks the runner, and here's the pitch.' You see how Hammer does it. You have to get some direction from Hammer."

I'm sure when I was managing, Hammer was giving Charlie plenty of direction. But that's just the way it was working for Charlie Finley. It was different—but it was always entertaining.

I worked for all kinds of owners, men and women. Joan Kroc in San Diego was a good gal, she just got some bad advice from some Mickey Mouse people around her. They would even go so far as to report me for smoking at Jack Murphy Stadium. There were some people who were jealous of my success. They didn't even want me to be called Trader Jack.

Some people close to her would forget that winning baseball games was the most important thing, not things like the San Diego Chicken.

I remember one game, the Chicken was all over the outfield doing some stunt where he was riding a horse. We were playing St. Louis. Whitey Herzog was the manager of the Cardinals, and his pitcher was pitching a no-hitter in the seventh inning. That inning the Chicken couldn't get the horse off the field. Whitey was upset, and I was upset.

After the game was over, I exploded. I raised hell about the Chicken and the next day I had to go into a meeting with some promotions people—Chicken backers.

They started saying the Chicken was a very important part of our ticket sales. I said, "Wait a minute. How many season ticket holders are in the Chicken package?"

"We've got about 230 Chicken packages."

"You mean to tell me you're bending over backwards for 230 Chicken packages? I'm the guy in charge of marketing here. What's important is what we do on that field. You sell tickets by winning games. That's what marketing is all about, winning games."

I got the Chicken off the field.

In 1984 the Padres won the pennant. The Chicken didn't win the pennant, the players did. I just reminded my critics who put that flag up there. It wasn't any Chicken, it was my players. I'm proud of that fact. I came on as interim GM in 1980, and four years later we won the pennant.

Joan's husband Ray was a wonderful guy, a lot like Ewing Kauffman in Kansas City. Their philosophy was pretty much the same. They rewarded people for success, just like Jeffrey Loria does in Florida.

When Ray was sick, I would go over to the hospital to visit with him. And he'd have his assistant there making notes for his McDonald's people. It was fascinating just listening to his comments. Ray would tell the assistant: "Write so-and-so a check for $25,000. Write this guy a check for $30,000, this guy a check for $50,000." Then he would explain to me why.

He'd say, "Jack, this guy here is my baker; he's the one who came up with this new cookie. We're having great success, and I want to reward him."

I never forgot Ewing Kauffman telling me the same thing. "We reward the people who helped in our success."

When we were trying to sign Steve Garvey as a free agent in San Diego in 1983, Atlanta was trying to sign him too. We had certain factions in our front office who said it was too much money to sign Garvey. Ray was in the hospital and Ballard Smith, the club president, and I went over to see him. I remember Ray saying, "Ballard, how are we coming along with Garvey?"

"Well I don't know, Ray, it's an awful lot of money."

Ray asked me, "What do you think, Jack?"

"I tell you, Ray, we have a good young club, but we don't have any experience. I don't think he is going to help us win it this year. But I think he is going to help these players mature and put us in a better position to win it in a year or two."

That's when Ray said, "Sign him, Ballard."

The next year we went over and had a little visit with him while we were negotiating with Goose Gossage, nearly the same scenario. "Ballard, how are you coming with Gossage?"

"Ray, it's too much money."

"What do you think, Jack."

"Ray, I think if we can get Gossage, we've got a chance to win the pennant."

"Sign him."

Unfortunately, Ray died before we won the pennant that year when we beat the Cubs in the playoffs. But those signings worked out just the way they were supposed to. They made it happen, and Ray made it happen by listening to my opinion. He knew I wasn't trying to smoke him. He knew I was just trying to make the team a pennant winner.

I even liked owners I didn't work for. In 1987, when I was GM of the Padres, Edward Bennett Williams, owner of the Orioles, called me in early October and said, "I was wondering if we could arrange a meeting in Washington here. Can you come to Washington on Monday to discuss this general manager's job?"

I said, "You're going to have to get permission from Chub Feeney." Feeney was the Padres president.

He said, "I already got it."

Funny, Chub had never told me that. So I flew to Washington and met with Mr. Williams and Larry Lucchino, who is now president of the Red Sox and was Mr. Williams' top man. I was prepared. I knew the Orioles system inside-out.

I've been through a lot of interviews and can tell when I've had a good interview. And this was a good one. I nailed it. So Mr. Williams asked what I wanted. I was making $300,000 with the Padres, and I said, "For me to make a switch from the West Coast back to the East Coast and all the stuff involved, knowing it's going to take me a few years to put this club back on it's feet, I'll need four years at $500,000 or five years at $400,000."

Mr. Williams said, "Let us think about it. I've got to go to L.A. and we'll get together in a week."

I went back, and a week later we met in L.A. He said, "Jack, you were the best interview we had, but I don't think I can meet your demands."

I said, fine, and they went out and hired Roland Hemond. I stayed in San Diego and eventually became GM and manager. In 1990 I got fired after new owners came in, but that's OK. It was only my 41st year in professional ball. I was just starting to get the hang of things.

CHAPTER 6

The Church of Baseball

Sometimes I'm quick to lose my temper with the umpires, but, overall, I'm a patient man. It took 14 years from the day I started college to the day I graduated, but I got it done. When you don't win your first World Series until you are almost 73, you learn what patience is all about.

I've been blessed, and I've been blessed for a long time. And I know that. I'm a Catholic, and faith has played a big role in my life.

I was a pretty good high school baseball player, an All-State player in New Jersey at St. Mary's High School. Baseball and basketball were my favorite sports, and in my senior year, 1948, the basketball team won the state championship. But a 5'9" guard wasn't going to go very far. Baseball was my future. There, a 5'9" catcher had a better chance.

The Pirates and the Red Sox came down to my house in South Amboy to sign me. My father had a seventh-grade education, and he told us, "I don't want you kids to have to work like I did—12, 18 hours a day to provide for your family. I want you to get a college education."

So he wouldn't let me sign. He wanted something bigger than the garage and taxi business for me, and I give him a lot of credit for that.

I had offers to go to Holy Cross and Fordham. I went to Holy Cross. It was 1948, and that was the year Bob Cousy, Joe Mullaney, and George Kaftan were on the basketball team. They had just won an NCAA Championship. I really wanted to play pro baseball, even though I liked college. Religion has always been important in guiding my life. It was important to my mom and dad, so I asked for help.

Every night that I went to the dining hall for dinner, I would pass the shrine of the Blessed Virgin Mary. Every night on my way back from dinner, I would stop and pray for about 20 minutes.

I asked the Blessed Virgin to intercede with the Good Lord to see if he couldn't in some way convince my father to let me sign a professional contract. Well, I went home for Christmas vacation, and the scouts came back and we met again. My father called me into another room and said, "You really want to play, don't you?" He caught me by surprise. He said, "I know you really want to go pro."

I saw my chance, and I told him that that was what I really wanted to do. "I love baseball, Dad."

"I'll tell you what," my father said. "I'll make a deal with you. If you promise me that you will get yourself a college education, I'll let you sign."

That was a piece of cake—even though it took until 1963 when I got my bachelor of science degree in physical education from Elon College. So my father let me sign, and that's how I got to be a professional ballplayer. I signed with the Pirates.

When you talk about the power of prayer, there it is. That is why I have such strong faith in the power of prayer. It's just like with this job. I was out for a couple of years and I prayed to St. Theresa. She's known as the "Prodigy of Miracles" in the Catholic Church. I prayed, I said, "I don't know what the Good Lord's plans are for me, but I sure would like to have one more chance to fulfill my career. I told the Good Lord I just wanted one more crack to manage. I didn't think I got a fair shake in Cincinnati to complete the job, and I wanted one more crack at it. And my prayers were answered. Boy, did they get answered. Winning a World Series ring is all I ever wanted.

The time I spent at home before getting this job was a blessing, too. I got to work with my grandson, Zachary Booker, who is now at North Carolina–Wilmington. I could throw him buckets of baseballs every day, so it all worked out for the best, helping him improve his baseball skills for college. That is the story of my life.

I've seen a lot of changes in the world. The year I was born the Empire State Building and the George Washington Bridge weren't even completed. That was 1930. I've had a lot of patience, but that's because I take each day as it comes, and I enjoy each day. Each day is a blessing; that's why I always say they call it "the present." Faith gets me through each day.

I truly believe the Good Lord is looking out for everybody, not just me. Every day I pray to St. Theresa, the Little Flower.

While I was praying every day during the early part of the 2003 season, I never dreamed that all this would happen. But then around August, I just had this feeling that we were going to win it all. I can't explain it, it was just a feeling I had. Then all of a sudden, here it is, my prayers were answered.

The role religion played in this was amazing. I'm not afraid of talking about God and the role he has played in my life, and that is something people want to hear. There are a lot of people out there like me, and I hear from them all the time. I'm always getting stuff in the mail. I received silver rosary beads and religious medals from nuns and priests all over the country.

I'm not a preacher, but I like to go to church every day, and I know the Good Lord. I've asked him to protect my players and guide those players and reward those players for the efforts that they put forth.

My prayers were answered in the NLCS against the Cubs, too. We went to Chicago and we were down 3–2. I went to church that morning and the priest, before Mass, walked up the aisle, tapped me on the shoulder, and said, "Nice going, good job, and good luck."

That's when I said, "We're in tonight." We were losing 3–0 in the eighth inning, but we had that unbelievable inning and won 8–3 to tie the series at three games apiece.

So now the whole season came down to one game. The next day I went to church again, and they said, "Today is the feast of St. Teresa of Avila."

Now, like I said, St. Theresa, the Little Flower, is the one I always pray to. She lets fall from heaven a shower of roses onto the earth, and she sure has showered the heck out of me. This was the other St. Teresa, but I just knew they would work together for me. And they did. I said right then and there, again, "We're in."

We were losing 5–3 in Game 7, but we came back to win 9–6. Once again, St. Theresa came through for me. The church I go to in Chicago is Holy Name Cathedral, and the pastor there, Father Dan Mayall sent me a nice note after we won the World Series. He wrote, "I hope to see you in Chicago again next year at Holy Name Cathedral."

He did, too, because going to church every day is important to me. During the World Series, I joked that more nuns were praying for me than for Joe Torre, whose sister is a nun.

In Hallandale Beach where I live in Florida, I go to 8:30 Mass at St. Matthews every morning. When I first started going there in 2003, they really didn't know me until about August. I was very quiet and wouldn't bother anybody. After we won the World Series, I was sitting in church the following Tuesday morning, and the pastor, Father Jim Quinn, made a great sermon, saying our win was a "lesson in dedication and perseverance and hard work of the team and of the owners and also of Mr. Jack McKeon."

All the people started clapping, it was unbelievable.

Going to church every day gives me peace of mind. It relaxes me. You leave and you feel good. You feel like you can accept any challenge that happens to you that day.

When I was in San Diego, the old mission church was right up the street from Jack Murphy Stadium. It was perfect. I could go to church and be back at the stadium in no time. That's the way I like it.

After I leave church, I go to the ballpark. I go, change, and then walk around the park for my daily exercise. A lot of times I'll pray the rosary while I'm walking. I'm praying the rosary and smoking my cigar. That's me.

Praying the rosary is a blessing. It gives me a feeling of security. I don't push my religion on anybody, I do it because I like to do it. It makes me feel good. But I sometimes talk to my players about it. A lot of ballplayers go to church.

When we're on the road or in spring training, I'll go to my center fielder, Juan Pierre, and say, "We've got to find a church tomorrow."

"Yeah, skip, it's Palm Sunday, we have to go."

So I'll go into town on a scouting trip and check the churches so I can let my guys know what time the Masses are. I'll come back and tell them, "OK, Mass is at 9:30. I'll meet you in the lobby and we'll go." I just point the players in the right direction and they like going, just like I do.

In New York at St. Agnes, a lot of times when I'm there I'll go up and take the collection. I've been doing it forever.

I remember one year in the minors, there was a left-handed pitcher named John Coakley. Because I was his catcher, we became friends. He loved baseball as much as I did. When he was growing up in Washington, D.C., he was a batboy for the Senators. He said the best player he ever saw was Joe DiMaggio, and he never forgot the impression Philadelphia A's manager Connie Mack made on him dressed in his suits. John later became a scout for the Senators.

We met in Gloversville, New York, in 1950. The Gloversville Glovers played in the old Canadian-American League. He's Protestant. We used to hang around together all the time, and I was going to church one day and he said, "I'd love to go to church."

"Come on, go with me," I said.

He said, "I'll go to church with you if you teach me the signs."

By signs, he meant how to bless himself. I said, "Just do what I do when I bless myself. It's just like watching the third base coach."

He did, and you know at the first Mass he went to, he met a girl named Joan. They wound up getting married. For 30 years they were married, until she passed away.

To this day, John and I are still friends, that's a blessing. Harry Dunlop was another guy. He was one of my coaches with the Royals, and he wanted a ride to the ballpark with me every day from the hotel. I said, "Look, I go to church at 6:30 in the morning." So I kept taking him to church, and he eventually converted. Harry coached with me in

San Diego and Cincinnati. And he's in Florida this season, too. And we go to church together.

People come up to me all the time and say they are going to church now because of me. I get letters from people saying, "You got me going to church every day." It makes me feel good to know I've made that kind of difference in someone's life.

One day, Pat Corrales, who was one of Bobby Cox's coaches with Atlanta, came up to me and said, "Jack, I just want to say I think what you are doing, talking about the importance of the Catholic Church in your daily life, is a great thing. I go to church, too, and I know exactly what you're saying."

That was great to hear.

Another day I was in church in Houston, and this lady gave me a note. The note said she needed a favor. Her boyfriend had been away from church for a number of years. She had tickets to the game Saturday night, and she told me where she was sitting. She wanted to know if I would invite the two to go to church. So I stopped by, and she introduced him to me. I said, "Hey, why don't you bring him to church tomorrow, and we'll go have coffee afterward?"

I saw her the next day at church, and she said it didn't work today, he had to go out of town. But he said he would take a rain check when he came back. She gave me a medal. I keep them all. My St. Anthony, St. Theresa, Padre Pio—people give me novenas.

I also got a Papal Blessing from Pope John Paul II. Jeffrey Loria got that for me. That means so much to me, and it shows you what kind of person Jeffrey is.

All of this just goes to show you about the power of prayer.

It's funny, I didn't realize it until after the World Series, but the Museum of Art in Fort Lauderdale hosted an exhibit: Saint Peter and the Vatican: The Legacy of the Popes. It was the largest Vatican collection to ever tour the United States. It included the drawings of Michelangelo. It came to South Florida right when we started getting hot at the end of August and stayed right through the World Series.

I had a lot of people praying for me, too, including my sister, Marge.

At the start of my managing career, I learned what was really important in this game and how you have to keep working for something you want.

My first managing job fell through with Hutchinson, Kansas. Branch Rickey had hired me to go out there, but the word never got to his farm director, and the next day the farm director hired someone else. So Rickey guaranteed I would manage Hutchinson the next season.

Even though I was disappointed about not getting the job, I was excited about the next season—and that's the way it is in baseball, you should always be excited about the next season, the next game, the next at-bat. You have to think ahead in baseball.

Rickey couldn't keep his promise with Hutchinson because the league folded over the winter. So back to North Carolina I went. I called Fayetteville, and they needed me to catch. And for once I was batting over my weight. I was hitting .285, and things were going good. But there was a limit to the number of veterans each team was allowed. I was the 16th, we were one over the limit.

At this point, the only place I thought I'd manage was the funeral home, where my father wanted me to work. That's why he sent me to college. He wanted me to be a funeral director. Then the Fayetteville owner asked if I wanted to manage. He said there might be an opening in two weeks.

"Sit tight and don't do anything," he told me.

I couldn't sit tight. I latched onto the Greensboro Red Sox as a catcher. They agreed to give me my release, though, when Fayetteville came through with the managing job.

That was a good plan, except I didn't get the chance to talk to the Fayetteville owner, and the first game I played was against Fayetteville. When the owner saw me catching for Greensboro, he blew his top and said, "Didn't I tell you to sit tight for two weeks?"

I finally calmed him down, and in a few weeks he did hire me as player/manager. But it didn't work out the way I thought it would.

What a group I had in front of me. My best pitcher worked construction and only showed up on days he pitched. It's a good thing I didn't need my closer until late in the game, because he worked over at Western Electric and couldn't make it to the games until the fifth or sixth inning. We also had a football coach who was late to games, and there were times we would only suit up 11 players.

I was worrying about all that until one night my second baseman, Bobby Lyons, got beaned with a fastball. It was scary. Bobby was a good player, and he was leading he league in hitting. He got hit in the head by one of the Giants' young hot-shot pitchers.

This was serious. You could see the indentation of the ball in his head. So after the game, I drove over to the hospital to see him, and the doctor said we had to rush him to a brain specialist over in Greensboro. I jumped in the ambulance with them, and they told me to keep him conscious.

I talked with Bobby all the way over to Greensboro. We got into the hospital, and they took him into the emergency room while I sat out in the lobby.

The doctor came out to me and said, "If we don't operate, he may not make it."

I tried to reach Bobby's wife; I tried to reach the owner of the club for permission to operate. At that point, the decision was in my hands.

This was no small decision, like putting on a steal or a hit and run, this was the biggest decision any manager could ever make. They said he could die in 12 hours without the surgery. At that point, Bobby was semiconscious. Surgery would give him a 50-50 chance of survival. When I whispered all that to him, he looked up at me and said, "That's a .500 average, Skip. I'll take that."

I'll never forget him going into the operating room. I was standing there and he was on the table. I don't think he was a religious guy, but he said, "Jack, pray for me."

And I did. I was praying and crying, and he made it through the operation. Eventually, he recovered. He never played another game in his life, but he lived.

I was thinking to myself, "So this is what managing is all about." While Bobby was out injured, the Fayetteville club waived him. Right then and there I knew it was a tough business. But I knew what I was getting into. Later in the season, I hurt my hand very badly and couldn't play for at least 10 days. The Fayetteville owner told me, "You don't play, we don't pay."

I got released, too. I learned a lot from that job, and I also learned that when God closes the door, he opens a window. Every day I went to church and prayed to St. Theresa.

I went back to college, and it wasn't long before a guy named Nick Mariana got in touch with me from Missoula, Montana. Branch Rickey came through for me this time. This guy had heard about me from Mr.

Rickey and how much I wanted to manage. His telegram said it all: "Need hustling young manager. Are you available?"

College could wait again. A door had closed in Fayetteville, but I was out the window, on my way to Missoula. Once again, my prayers were answered.

CHAPTER 7

Times of a Lifetime

Hang around me for a while and you'll see there is rarely a day that goes by when I don't mention Missoula, Montana.

There was no place like it. We were the Missoula Timberjacks.

And I wasn't even the fastest-talking catcher in the league. I managed there for three years, starting in 1956, and I also caught. There was a catcher from Boise named Bob Uecker. Despite all the jokes about his career and how bad he was in the majors, I could tell right away that he had big-league ability.

If you run into Uecker today, he can still sing the Missoula fight song that they made up for us: "Timberjacks, Hurry Back."

I'm lucky I lived through my experience in Missoula. We had a trap door right on the field, about the same size as a cellar door. We had to lift that door up to come out of the clubhouse and go into our dugout. That's how we had to go back into the clubhouse, too. One day I sent one of my pitchers to the showers. Pitchers can be pretty emotional when they leave games.

I know in the big leagues there are some places where the guard posted outside the clubhouse door is instructed to open that door when a pitcher is coming his way after being taken out of a game. They don't want the pitcher knocking the door off its hinges.

So our pitcher went to the clubhouse and left the trap door wide open and nobody noticed. There was a pop fly, I went chasing after it and right down the steps I went. Bam!

Uecker tells the story all the time. He says, "Yeah, that Jack McKeon, he was one out-of-sight player."

So many things happened in the minors that you wouldn't see in a major league park, and I think that's why I loved being there. And when people say I'm wired for baseball, they're not kidding.

In 1962 in Vancouver I wired my pitcher for communication purposes. Basically, I made him into a walkie-talkie on the mound. This was long before cell phones. I've always figured, why not try something new? I try to get every edge I can get on the ballfield as long as it's legal. Why not give the fans a show in the process?

George Bamberger, who went on to manage the Brewers and Mets, was my coach and a pitcher. I was tired of having the other pitchers not following instructions, so I was determined to do something about it. We had just lost a game because I knew Preston Gomez, the opposing manager, was going to squeeze. I ordered four straight pitchouts, so what did my pitcher do? He threw a curve for a strike and then another curve. The batter bunted, the run scored from third. We lost.

I'd had enough of that. So I asked a couple of sportswriters if they knew of anyone who could hook me up with an electronics guy so I could talk to my pitcher and catcher right there on the field. One writer did, and his electronics expert told me he could set up the pitcher. I had pockets sewn right into the inside of his shirt so I could fit the receiver in there.

We were playing Spokane in a doubleheader, and I had it all set up for the second game. I walked out to the dugout with my electronics bag. We'd already tested the transmitter and receiver, and it worked from 200 yards. Now we were going to use it to pick off guys at first. The only problem was that I hadn't told my first baseman, a guy named Ray Looney, who went on to become an FBI agent.

That was unfortunate. When I saw the runner at first with a big lead, Bamberger, or "Bambi" as we called him, didn't even have to look, I just said, "Throw!" and he wheeled and fired—and hit Ray right in the chest.

Years later when I became manager of the Kansas City Royals, we opened the new stadium there. I was sitting in the dugout an hour before the game during batting practice, and two FBI agents came down and slapped the cuffs on me.

"You gotta go with us," they said.

I was scared to death. Ray, the practical joker, who was based in Waterbury, Connecticut, called the FBI office in Kansas City and said, "Do me a favor, slap the cuffs on this guy."

They were taking me out. I didn't know what was going on. But they finally let me go. Ray got me good that night.

But Bambi was picking off guys left and right once Ray knew what was coming. If the runner got too big a lead, I'd yell "Throw!" and we'd get him. The papers had a field day with it. The headline was VANCOUVER MOUNTIES MAKE BASEBALL HISTORY.

The next week we went to Spokane. I called the opposing GM and told him to get some electronic equipment so that he could act like he was going to intercept my transmissions. We came into town and the headline read: WIRELESS MOUNTIES, MEN FROM OUTER SPACE.

So they set up a table with all kinds of instruments on it to intercept our transmissions, even a little satellite dish. I had Gerry Arrigo, who later pitched for the Reds, on the mound.

I had this transistor radio along with my transmitter, and I said to Jerry, "How would you like a little rock n' roll music while you're warming up?" As you can tell, I was ahead of my time. Now they do that in all the parks, play music during batting practice and warm-ups, chosen by the players.

Gerry said, "Sure," so I turned on Red Robin's *Rock N' Roll Show* while Gerry was out there pitching. I got no reaction from the "spy" table, so I knew they weren't picking us up. About the fifth or sixth inning, I figured I would keep them honest, so I called out, "Cab 35, go to Ridpath Hotel." That's where we were staying. Again, I didn't get any reaction, so I knew they weren't picking us up.

Everywhere we went, this story was getting bigger and bigger. They were calling us everything under the sun: The Electronic Mounties, The Space Cadets, The Wireless Kids. I was way ahead of my time.

We were getting great publicity, so I figured I might as well take advantage of it. We were going into San Diego next. I went down to an automotive shop and bought a car antenna. I got a helmet, and at the top of it, I drilled a hole and put the antenna in there. I put call letters on the helmet and went to coach third base with the helmet and antenna.

It was great. The fans loved it.

Now this night Bambi was pitching, but I didn't have him wired. But nobody knew this. He got knocked out in the fourth inning, and while we were both walking off the mound, the fans behind us were yelling, "Hey Bambi, you tuned into the wrong station."

When we went to Hawaii, I put the receiver in Bambi's shirt and sent him over to the batting cage before the game. I told him to get into a conversation with their catcher, Charlie White, who used to catch for Milwaukee. I figured we'd have some fun with Charlie. So he was over there talking to Charlie, and I had the transmitter in the dugout. I said to White, "Hey, you big fat goat." He didn't know who was talking to him. We had that guy going crazy.

I kept everything, and the next year I was managing in Dallas–Ft. Worth. One night I got thrown out of a game by Russ Goetz, who later umpired in the American League. Bambi was my coach, so I took my transmitter, set it up in the stands, and told Bambi what to do while he was managing.

Goetz saw me in the stands, but he had no idea what I was doing. He didn't know I was talking to my coach in the dugout. He thought I was crazy, sitting there just talking to myself. It turns out I was the first guy who electronically managed a game after being thrown out.

As you can tell, I'm not afraid to get in an argument. I've been in the middle of all kinds of baseball brawls. We were playing Winston-Salem back in 1968. We hit a couple of home runs, and they started throwing at my hitters. I was riding this pitcher from third base, and the third baseman said to me, "Why don't you shut the hell up."

I said, "If you don't shut your mouth, I'm going to kick the hell out of you."

Just about that time the pitcher was winding up, and the third baseman said, "You ain't got the guts."

With that I took off after him. My hitter singled up the middle while the third baseman and I were out there slugging away, but no one saw us because they were watching the ball.

Fighting was part of the game back then. One night I decked Doc Edwards at home plate. I was managing Wilson in the Carolina League, and we were playing Burlington in Wilson. I was coaching third, and there was a play at the plate. My runner slid across the plate and was safe. Doc got the ball late and jumped across the plate and kneed my runner. The guy was laid out. I ran in and said, "You know, Doc, that garbage is uncalled for. I ought to knock you on your tail."

The next thing I said was "I think I will." So we had a free-for-all at home plate.

The next week we had to go to Burlington. I talked to the general manager and the manager there, Pinkie May. That was the year that Ingemar Johansson was the heavyweight champion.

I said to the GM, "If you really want to draw a crowd, why don't you put a ring up in front of home plate and announce that Pinkie and I are going to go a couple rounds?" Nobody would have gotten hurt, it would have been great. But Pinkie wouldn't go for it. He said that would have been a sellout. What Pinkie didn't understand is that back then in the minor leagues, you had to sell. That's how you sell out.

I sold and sold. One time I was asked to set something up with the Tulsa club by their owner, A. Ray Smith. Warren Spahn was his manager. We drew about 1,500 people, and after the game I went up to Smith's lounge at the ballpark. He said, "You've got to help me out now." A. Ray was a little bit like Bill Veeck, the great baseball showman.

There was a doubleheader the next day, and Smith was a great one to have his organist play music while the opposing pitcher was pitching. I said, "You know you've done that before, and I raised hell. We can do that, but we're going to do it on my cue. We're not going to mess around and blow a game. I'll give you the sign when I come from third base after the inning."

So the next day we went ahead 5–0 in the first game of the doubleheader. It was a seven-inning game. I knew we were going to hold this game, so I gave him the sign.

The pitcher was Monty Montgomery and in came the music. I let him throw one pitch, and I didn't say anything. The second pitch came and the music was still playing, so I bolted out of the dugout and raised hell with the umpire. The umpire told the guy to shut the music off. He stopped playing.

The next pitch he started up again with the music and I was out of the dugout again, raising hell. Warren Spahn didn't know anything about the setup; the general manager didn't know anything about it; the umpires didn't know anything about this; only the opposing owner and I knew about it. We were arguing, and A. Ray was sitting alongside the organist and told him to keep playing. Their general manager, Hugh Finnery, finally came on the field, and they were ready to forfeit the game. Finally, the guy stopped the music.

The next morning I had two television stations doing interviews with me. They asked me why I didn't like the music. I told them I never took music appreciation in college. Then they made a big deal out of it and told all the fans to come out with musical instruments.

The next night we had about 4,500 people out there with horns and drums and every kind of musical instrument, and they were raising hell all because of our plan.

It didn't hurt my pitcher, though. We won both games.

I remember one night one of my pitchers was so bad that after I took him out of the game and brought in the reliever, Steve Jones, I said to Steve. "Hey, walk around here, to the front of the mound. Walk this way."

He said, "Why?"

I pointed to the ground and said, "Because I don't want to step in any of this crap the other guy left all over the place."

I always did things my way. My first spring training was in New Orleans in 1949. I took the train there, and it was my first time in a Pullman car. Even though I was a rookie minor leaguer, I wasn't going to stop playing the role of a professional ballplayer.

There were a couple of other ballplayers on the train, too. We didn't know where to go and didn't know anything about New Orleans. But I used to listen to the radio all the time, and I always remembered them saying, "Here's Tommy Dorsey and his band from the beautiful Hotel Roosevelt in New Orleans."

So we got to New Orleans, jumped in a cab, and I told the cabbie to take us to the Hotel Roosevelt. We had all our baseball gear with us, and when we walked in the door, all the people were dressed in tuxedos.

They didn't want any low-rent ballplayers there. They directed us to the door and another hotel down the street. Tommy Dorsey wasn't playing there, but the cockroaches were. That was my welcome to pro ball. I may not have always stayed in the best hotels through the years, but I always had the best time.

CHAPTER 8

Sixth Sense

Some people say I can see and smell a ballplayer from a mile away. I agree with them.

One of the big reasons the Marlins won the National League pennant and the World Series in 2003 was because of the rapid progress of young Miguel Cabrera, who is just a tremendous kid. Our scouts and development people did a great job with him.

I took over the team in May, but I had my eye on Cabrera long before that. Like any other retired person, I went down to Florida for a little vacation during spring training. I went to Jupiter to see my old friend Bill Beck, traveling secretary for the Marlins.

I was still out of a job, but I wanted to catch some sun and watch some baseball. It just so happened that the Marlins were playing a split squad game against Cincinnati, my old team. I sat in the bleachers, smoking a cigar and enjoying the game. All of a sudden I saw this Cabrera kid, and he had one heck of a day, hitting the ball everywhere.

So I got on the phone and called my son, Kasey, who's with Colorado. Remember, I wasn't working for anybody, so I figured I'd do a little birddog work for Kasey. I told him if you ever make a deal with the Marlins, make sure to get this kid Cabrera.

He said, "Dad, I know all about Cabrera, we had him in our Dominican Academy with the Reds and they wouldn't give me the money to sign the kid. We could have signed him for $800,000 at the time. They only gave me $500,000, that was it."

As you can see, Kasey's got a great eye for talent, too.

Cabrera wound up signing with the Marlins. If the Reds had spent the money when Kasey wanted them do, they would have had a bargain in Cabrera. That's the way this game goes. When a scout sees someone he really loves, the team has to have faith in his judgment and have the confidence to give him what he needs to sign the player.

When I did take over the Marlins, one of the first things I did was make Cabrera an everyday player. Cabrera is really a third baseman. He had to play outfield because that was the only spot we had for him. You can't be afraid to play a talent like that. Too many teams don't move the really good players up fast enough.

The backbone of any successful team is the scouts. I've always enjoyed my time with the scouts, and through the years, I spent a lot of time scouting with my brother, Bill, and Dick Hager.

We were family. In fact, when Hager would call my house, Carol used to answer the phone and say, "Jack, your brother's on the line."

That's how close we were. He was my traveling companion, and we used to have a ball in Puerto Rico, where we picked up some pretty good players in Roberto and Sandy Alomar, Benito Santiago, and some others.

My secretary with the Padres was Rhoda Polley. Rhoda also moon-lighted as a real estate agent. So Dick and I were in Puerto Rico one year, and we were driving over from San Juan to Arricibo. We went through some of these old back roads, and there were these buildings about ready to fall down.

There was a For Sale sign on one building. Dick got his camera out, took a picture of the building, and sent it to Rhoda. He said, "Hey, see if you can negotiate a deal for this."

Then we went down to Arricibo, and there was an old sign out there: "Rooms for Rent, Pedro's Motel." The sign was hanging on one chain, so Dick took a picture of that and sent it to Padres president Dick Freeman and wrote, "Dick, see where we're staying. We're saving the club money."

Dick and I go all the way back to 1962 and Vancouver. That year we took a great picture at the Frazier Arms Hotel for the *Vancouver Sun*. Dick had a birddog scout named George Oikawa, and we had two players we signed. We got a real birddog to point at the players as we stood there.

Scouts are a special breed. One of my favorites of all-time was Hughie Alexander. Everybody knew him as Uncle Hughie.

Hughie was a great talker, and he knew what he was doing. He was a good player, too, but when he was 20, he lost his hand in an oil-drilling accident in the off-season. He used to like to say, "After that, nothing could ever hurt me."

Hughie was from Oklahoma, and he would drive everywhere looking for players. One of his favorite stories was about going to a high school in Oklahoma where he heard there was a top prospect. He wrote the kid's name down on a piece of paper, went to the high school, and checked with the principal. The principal said the kid was injured in football and had arthritis, and besides, the high school didn't even have a baseball team. Hughie left without ever seeing the player. When he got back to his car, he crumbled up the piece of paper and tossed it away, watching it blow away in the wind.

"You know what the name was on the paper?" Hughie would say, years later, telling the story to anyone who would listen.

"Mickey Mantle. I can still see that piece of paper blowing across that parking lot."

Hughie was one of my counterparts with the Phillies and the Cubs. We were very close and put together many deals because of our honest relationship with one another.

We would keep each other posted on what we were trying to do. If we didn't have a match with a team, Hughie could jump in and help make it a three-way deal, or I could help him. They call that networking now.

Dick Hager and my brother, Bill, were my two major league scouts. I leaned heavily on both. My brother scouted the American League, and Dick scouted the National League.

In New Jersey my name is pronounced "Mc-Kune," but when I went down south to play ball, they started calling me "Mc-Ke-on." After a while I got tired of trying to correct people, so I just let it go.

Now whenever my brother and I are introduced at some function, he's Bill "Mc-Kune" and I'm Jack "Mc-Ke-on." Other than our last name, we're usually on the same page.

Whenever I was making a trade, I would send Bill and Dick out. If I was talking to the Yankees, I'd send Dick to Columbus to look at their Triple-A club and my brother Bill to look at the Double-A club so we had a pretty good background on all the players involved. I would also go out myself and look at the players.

I had tremendous faith in their evaluations, but I still wanted to see these players with my own eyes. I wanted to get a chance to see what they were talking about. I also had Joe Lutz and Vince Valecci, two great baseball guys who did part-time work for us in scouting. We didn't pay them much, but I would take them to spring training for a week or so, all expenses paid. They also were two very good kibitzers. To be a good scout, you have to be a good talker.

One year in Yuma, Arizona, I kept saying how I couldn't wait to get rid of Joe and Vince after they had been there a week. They had a flight at 6:00 in the morning, so I said I'd take them to the airport.

We were driving down the street at 6:00 in the morning, and I was blowing the horn the whole way through town, yelling, "Yeah, I'm getting these guys out of town. I can't wait to get them out of town." I got them to the airport and went in with them. All these people were waiting there, and I said, "Hey, make sure these guys stay on the plane. Get them out of here."

Yuma has a small airport, and the gates are outside. I climbed up on the fence and yelled, "Make sure you get them on the plane."

Vince lives in Philadelphia, and one time he came to the airport there to pick up Ballard Smith, president of the Padres, and me. He brought his older car, and Ballard really didn't know Vince well. He didn't know that Vince and I always were kidding with each other, we were old Air Force buddies. So I got in the front seat, Ballard got in the back, and I say to Vince, "Geez, the president of the club, how can you pick him up in this piece of junk, this garbage pile?"

Vince starts yelling back at me, "You no-good, ungrateful son of a gun. I saved you in the service, I protected you in the service and everything else, and this is the thanks I get."

We went back and forth, and Ballard didn't have any idea that we did this all the time. He thought it was for real. That was the fun stuff we did all the time.

As a scout, I loved watching young players develop, and I've had all kinds of characters. John Kruk was one of those, no question about it, and now you see him every night on TV on *Baseball Tonight*. I knew a long time ago he was one of a kind when we drafted him with the Padres.

The thing about Kruk was that he could hit falling out of bed. He was a little chubby guy in the minor leagues, and no one ever gave him a chance. No one ever thought, even though he hit, that he could play. He was classified as a weak first baseman. We played him in the outfield and at first base, and eventually he wound up playing first base.

People always ask me, "What did you see in that guy?" The key to good scouting is seeing what other scouts don't see or don't want to see. With John, I had to admire the guy because he made himself into a pretty good player, he was a gamer. And he's doing the same thing on TV now. He's got street smarts, baseball smarts, and he tells it like it is. Sometimes you don't like what he says, but it's like the time I traded him, he took it personally. A lot of guys, they hold it against you, like you don't like them. It's not personal, it's business.

When I traded John, I put him on the right team for him at the right time, the Phillies. John played hard, he was a little goofy at times, but you couldn't take away the fact that the guy had so much desire and determination to succeed, and that's what I saw. When he got the opportunity, he jumped on it. He always had fun in the game. The more experience he got, the better he became. In his early days, he was having too much fun, but as he progressed and established himself, he took this thing more seriously. And he really hit it off with Tony Gwynn. They were good for each other.

In 1981 we signed Kruk, Tony Gwynn, Kevin McReynolds, and Greg Booker. Booker's my son-in-law. Everybody but McReynolds was at Walla Walla, Washington. We had the strike that year, and I sent

Clyde McCullough, one of our major league coaches, up there to work with them, because Clyde was so good with young players.

I went up to watch them work out, and I took the staff out to dinner. We were sitting around, shooting the bull, and I said, "How many prospects do we have here?"

One of the guys said to me, "We've only got one. And that's the shortstop."

Clyde jumped up right away and said, "Hey wait a minute. What are you guys looking at? I can see at least three players here that are prospects, Booker, Kruk, and Gwynn."

Clyde was right on the money. He had a feel for young players, he had a vision. A lot of times, managers and coaches judge guys in a Rookie League on how they're doing, and they don't see the big picture. They don't see the talent because it's not performing like they hoped it would. A kid who is having a good year with the numbers is looked upon as a prospect, while a guy who is having a mediocre year, they don't consider a prospect. They don't look at the long range and say, "Hey, this guy, when he puts it together is going to be a hell of a player."

Don't just look at the numbers. Look at the future. Look at what the kid is going to be.

When I see a prospect, I just have this inner feeling. One year there was a kid at New Orleans named Augie Schmidt who hit about 35 home runs, and our guys were raving about him. I went down to take a look at him and said, right away, "Uh-uh, not for me."

Something didn't hit me right. Our guys wanted to take him over McReynolds or Joe Carter, but I didn't like him for that pick. I wanted McReynolds or Joe Carter. Joe Carter went No. 2, and that left us with McReynolds.

But I wanted Tony Gwynn, too. Now it was a question of Billy Long or Tony Gwynn. I hadn't seen Billy Long, so I asked all the scouts, "All you guys telling me Billy Long is better than Tony Gwynn?" They said, "Yes."

I said, "Fine, I'll go along with your word, but Tony Gwynn is going to be our third pick, regardless."

Tony was a basketball player at San Diego State, and a lot of scouts didn't see him play baseball. I saw San Diego State play 15 games, and all the scouts were in early because they started playing early in San Diego. Most of the scouts didn't go back later in the season. That was a big mistake. They missed the best player on the team.

We happened to play San Diego State in an exhibition game, and we had two of our better pitchers on the mound. Gwynn doubled, tripled, and ran the bases like he had eyes in the front, side, and back of his head.

I said, "Look at the instincts on this guy." I asked, "Who the hell is that guy?" And their athletic director told me, "That's Tony Gwynn."

I said, "I've seen San Diego State play 15 times, and I've never seen him before." And he said, "He just came out. Basketball season just ended, and he only had a week to work out."

He was the best player on the team. You've got to go back in scouting, you have to be persistent.

I remember going to see Shawon Dunston when he was a high school player in New York. I was with the Padres, and I had a limo pick up me and Hall of Fame writer Phil Collier from the *San Diego Union*, at our hotel. We went out to Brooklyn and watched Dunston. He didn't do anything in that game, but right away you saw the talent. You saw him take batting practice, you saw the fluidness. I liked him.

I saw Darryl Strawberry out in L.A. He struck out twice, walked twice, didn't hit a foul ball, but you could see the potential there. In high school, the big hitters like Strawberry either get walked by the opposing pitchers, or they are so hungry for a hit, they swing at anything.

If you're talking about first impressions, the best guy I ever saw in that respect was Steve Garvey. I recommended that we draft Steve Garvey for the Twins back in 1965—and we did. The best two high school hitters I saw when I was scouting high schools were Garvey and Richie Zisk. I tried to draft Zisk with the Twins, but our superscouts didn't like him.

Garvey was a third baseman then, and everybody said, "He can't move, he's going to get heavy."

What got heavy was his batting average, he was a .294 hitter over 19 years in the big leagues. There was something there I saw in him when he was a kid. That something turned out to be talent, and to his credit, he became the player that I thought he would be.

People always point to drafting Tony Gwynn as my best draft. That was in 1981. You could see he had the stroke and that sixth sense about the game. He was the best player out there, but I didn't know he was going to be as good as he was.

Twenty years later, Tony wound up with 3,141 hits and a lifetime .338 average, and he's going to be in the Hall of Fame. More than the numbers, Tony's a great person, and it's great to see him now coaching at San Diego State. Tony is one of the greatest players and people I've ever been associated with, and he's got one of the best laughs in all the game.

If you have a funny story to tell, make sure you tell it when Tony is standing there.

I never liked relying on a radar gun as a scout. Sometimes a pitcher can just pitch. Look at Jim Kaat—it's not always about how fast they throw. Look at Tom Glavine. You change speeds and you drive a batter to drink. Nowadays all you hear is, "This guy's got a great arm."

Yeah, but can he get anybody out?

Can he get the ball over the plate? Who gives a darn if they throw 95? Give me the guy who throws 89 and can spot his pitches.

One of my favorite times of the year as a GM was the Rule V Draft. That's how I picked up Alan Wiggins, who played second on the Padres team that won the pennant in 1984. I saw Wiggins play in one game. We had a farm club in Reno, and I saw this guy on the other team get a base hit, steal second, and steal third. The next time up he bunted, stole second, and stole third, and I said, "This is an intriguing kid."

After the season was over, we were getting ready for the Rule V Draft. I was scanning the rosters. The Albuquerque roster was the Dodgers farm club. I went down the list of all the players, and the last name on the list was Wiggins. I said, "Wiggins. I remember him." I told my scouting people to get the reports on him.

"Is this the guy who stole 106 bases?"

They said, "Yeah."

There were four scouting reports we had on him. Three said he was no prospect, and one said he was marginal at best.

I said, "We're going to draft him. I don't give a damn what anybody thinks about taking a guy out of Class A. He can stay in the big leagues." In the meantime, I talked to Al Campanis with the Dodgers who had had Wiggins, and I said, "Do you want him back?"

He said, "Why, do you want to give me a player?"

"I'll be glad to give you a player," I said. So I gave him a Double-A or Triple-A player to let me send Wiggins back to the minors to develop. I was able to send him to Triple-A Hawaii, and he wasn't in

Hawaii for more than a month and a half before I had him in the big leagues. Bip Roberts was the same way with the Rule V Draft, and I nearly got Bobby Bonilla. In a game in Double-A, Bip and Bonilla collided and got hurt. I grabbed Roberts in the first round and was going to take Bonilla in the second because he was hurt. Everything went smoothly. I got Roberts in the first round, but in the second round, the pick before us, the White Sox grabbed Bonilla. That's the way it goes.

In spring training writers always ask me, "Who's going to make the team?"

I always say, "The players will decide it for me. If you put them out there enough they'll make the decision for me."

I've always been good about making a decision. I even scouted myself. When I was in the minors, we didn't have any batting coaches, so I'd evaluate myself.

I really couldn't help myself much; you can only do so much with so much talent. I remember I used to change my batting stance a lot. One time I copied Gil McDougald's stance. He was a Yankee who used to crouch over like he had a backache. That stance gave the fans a headache. Fans saw me way bent over, and they'd scream, "Take a nap somewhere else, McKeon!"

I finally quit playing in 1959 after I scouted myself and realized I was done. I'd been a player/manager since 1955. I called the office one day, and they didn't want a player/manager. I was too old, I was 27.

Lee Stange was pitching that night and he threw two curveballs. He had a nasty curve that hit home plate and bounced up over my head to the screen. Two in three innings. The next day I picked up the paper and they'd given me passed balls. I said that's enough, they really want me out of here, and I retired. I was too old 45 years before they said I was too old.

That turned out to be the best move I ever made, because I always knew talent and now I could hone that skill. Even after my managing days are over, I'd love to stay in the game scouting. The way I figure it, either you can see talent or you can't and it doesn't matter if you're 20 or if you're 80.

CHAPTER 9

Travelin' Man

In 1954 I was a backup catcher for Burlington. Reality had set in. I had seen great catchers like Yogi Berra and Roy Campenella. I knew I was not going to make the big leagues as a player.

More and more, my thoughts turned to managing, and in 1954 Branch Rickey offered me a job managing in Clinton, Iowa. But once he found out I was still going to college, he said, "No, I'm not going to keep you from a college education."

We were in first place, and I was going to marry Carol. So a little later in the season, he called and said he wanted me to go and play in Hutchinson, Kansas. I had to say yes—it was Branch Rickey. But then he told the Burlington owner Red Fowler, "I just wanted to see if he would do me a favor. Tell Jack he's going out there to manage."

I went out and met the team in Ponca City, Oklahoma, but I was told I wouldn't take over managing for about a week, so I was put back behind the plate.

I was reading the paper one morning and I couldn't believe what I saw. The headline read: LARRY DORTON NAMED HUTCHINSON MANAGER.

Larry Dorton? I was the new manager, not Larry Dorton. It turns out there was a major league mix-up. Rickey never told his farm director that I was going out to manage Hutchinson, and the farm director hired Larry Dorton.

It probably was a good thing I wasn't hired as manager. The league folded over the winter. The next season I started managing in Fayetteville, where I was a player/manager. Each of the next 10 years I managed in the minors. I took a three-year break to scout for the Twins and then it was five more years managing in the minors. Nearly a quarter of a century from when I started in 1949, I would finally make it to the major leagues in 1973 to manage the Royals.

That's what I mean when I say you have to have perseverance in life. And you've got to have a sense of humor.

When I first started in the minors, we didn't have cars. If we wanted to get somewhere, we'd have to hitchhike. We'd hitchhike all over the place. Two or three of us would be walking together, and people would stop, pick us up, and take us to the park or wherever we were going.

We had some fun with it, too. One of my first managers told me, "Never tell anybody you're a ballplayer. Tell them you are a foundry worker or something." So people would stop and pick us up, we'd get in the car and, invariably, the driver would say, "So, what do you guys do?"

I'd sit back and say, "We're down here working for the government. We're checking out the engines on these ships."

Looking back on it, the guys who picked us up must have thought we weren't too smart—"Here they got these good jobs and they're hitchhiking."

One day, Bill Wiltrout, another guy, and I were hitchhiking in North Carolina, and some guy picked us up and said, "What do you guys do?"

A couple of my first jobs in baseball: in my crouch for the Gloversville (New York) Glovers in 1950, and striking a pose a few years later for the Missoula (Montana) Timberjacks, the origin of many of my favorite baseball stories.

That's me and my mother, Anna McKeon, relaxing at home (above) and a few years later when I was managing in Oakland.

Visiting with my two daughters (top, from left), Kelly and Kristi, in Atlanta in 1964, and then strolling with the whole family in 1973.

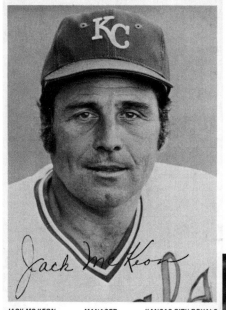

Three of my managerial stops along the way: as a rookie with Kansas City in 1973; my first year with the A's, in 1977; and then back in the dugout in San Diego in the late eighties, after a 10-year hiatus.

Jack McKeon

JACK MC KEON   MANAGER   KANSAS CITY ROYALS

I took another six-year break from managing, then took over the Reds from 1997 to 2000.

I was hired by the Marlins early in the 2003 season (above), and by October we were facing Joe Torre and the Yankees in the World Series.

My wife Carol and I got to hoist the World Series trophy (top) after our win, and then the team paid a visit to the White House a few months later.

Really, I feel like I'm just getting started . . .

I said, "We're Christian Science workers."

I was looking out the window because I didn't want to laugh. I said, "We're on our way to Elon. A couple of our brothers have gone astray, and we want to meet with them and see if we can't bring them back. We were at North Carolina State yesterday, we try to go around to these college towns and keep our brothers on the right path."

We finally got to the place where we were going, and I said, "You can let us off here."

He pulled up to the corner and said, "I believe in Christ, too. Now you guys pray for me."

Even to this day when I get in a cab, I have some fun when I'm riding with my coaches. One day we got in a cab in San Francisco and the cabbie asked, "Where you from?"

I said, "Alaska," and he said, "Me too. Whereabouts?" There are only two towns I know about up there—Fairbanks and Anchorage. He said, "I'm from Anchorage." I told him I was from Fairbanks, and we started talking.

Now, I've never been to Alaska or any of the places I tell people I live. Winnipeg is another one of my favorites. I got in a cab one day, and the cabbie asked where I'm from. I said, "Winnipeg." He said, "Really? I used to live there."

So I ran with it. I said, "I've been gone a few years, but you know on Main Street over there by the theater." He said, "Yeah."

And I said, "Well I used to live right behind there. One block up."

He went for it and said, "Oh yeah, I remember that place."

Hell, all towns have a Main Street and a theater.

In Philadelphia I had a good one going, too. Some coaches and I got in the cab, and the cabbie said, "What do you fellas do?"

"We're with the Environmental Soil Agency," I told him. "We're going out to this new stadium here in Philadelphia, Citizens Bank Park, to check out the soil to see if it has the right mixture of clay and sodium. We just came in from San Diego, where we checked out their new stadium."

"That must be a pretty interesting job," he said. "I never paid that much attention to the soil."

I didn't either. I was just throwing all kinds of stuff at him. I didn't know what I was talking about. The coaches were in the back seat laughing. I don't know if it helps the team to play better baseball, it's just another way to keep things loose, and we've sure had a lot of success against the Phillies since I've been here.

I've seen some crazy cab drivers in my day, too—and I should know, I was one of them. One of the craziest rides I ever took was with Cedric Tallis, the GM of the Royals, when I was managing in Kansas City. It was during spring training, and we were at a dinner hosted by the governor for all the spring training teams. We gave a ride to the owner of the Tokyo Giants. Tallis was really flying down the back roads of Florida—we were going from St. Petersburg to Fort Myers—and the Tokyo owner was scared to death. He had his feet pushed against the dashboard, he was so scared. We finally made it to Fort Myers safely, and the poor guy was shaking. We dropped him off, and the next day I saw him at the ballpark. I said, "Hey, how are things going?"

He said, "No more. No more. No ride with him." He said, of Tallis, "Kamikaze driver."

I've never had more fun with one player than with Chuck Weatherspoon, good old "Spoonie." One year on the last day of the season, we were in Vancouver, staying at the Frazier Arms. I got down to the lobby early on the day we were going to check out, and I called his room. I disguised my voice and said, "Mr. Weatherspoon, this is Hertz Rental Car. We're still waiting for you to return the car you rented."

"I didn't rent no car," he yelled into the phone.

I said, "Now, sir, it has your name right here. We're just going to take it to the authorities. You have to remember, you're in Canada, and you are not going to get out of this country if I file this report that you have stolen this car."

So we went to the park and had two security guys there. I told them to come down to the clubhouse and ask for me when Weatherspoon came in. "I'll go to the door, so he can hear, and I'll say, 'No, Mr. Weatherspoon, he's not here yet.'"

So they came down, and I covered for him. When they left I went up to his locker and said, "Spoonie, what the hell is going on?"

"Skip, they're trying to accuse me of stealing a rental car."

He was not starting that day, anyway, so I told him to go hide somewhere and I'd try to protect him.

The security guards came to the door again. "Is Mr. Weatherspoon in here?"

"No, he's not here."

"Well, you tell him there is no way he that he can leave Canada. We'll get him at the border if we have to."

During the game, he was in the dugout. He had his jacket pulled up, and I had the security guard poke his head in the dugout and ask, "Is Weatherspoon in there?"

Around the fourth inning, I decided to put him in the game. He said, "Skip, I can't go in there, they're looking for me."

I said, "No, it's all taken care of, I straightened it out for you." Then he relaxed. He went in there and got a couple of hits. To this day, I never told him it was all a setup.

Spoonie lives in Texas now. We had some great times together. He always used to try to get his age reduced. He was the first Danny Almonte. He's probably about four years younger than I am, and one year it would say in the paper, "28-year-old Chuck Weatherspoon," and the next year he tried to go to 25.

I told him he should have just tried to get one year younger or stay the same.

One day in 1964 I was managing Atlanta, and we were going to play a bunch of prisoners at the Atlanta State Penitentiary in an exhibition game. We're walking down the corridor, and there were a bunch of cells. We were dressed in our uniforms.

I went over and started talking to the prisoners. I said, "Hey, where you guys from?" They told me, we talked a while, and then I asked for a favor. I said, "Hey, I got a guy coming in here. His name is Chuck Weatherspoon, his nickname is Spoonie. He's from Pineland, Texas. I'll call him over here and you guys holler, 'Hey, Spoonie, Spoonie!' Make like you know him. You tell him that you went to school with him. And then I'm going to ask you how old he is, and you're going to say, 'He's got to be about 35.'"

So Spoonie came in, the guys called him over, and I said, "You know Spoonie?"

"Oh yeah, I went to high school with him," one of the guys said.

I said, "You're just the guy I want to see. Tell me, how old is he?"

The con plays the con perfectly, saying, "Well, we went to school together. He's got to be 33, 34 years old."

Spoonie yelled, "I don't know these guys," and he went out into the field and played the game. When the game was over, I said to Spoonie, "Get all the helmets together Spoonie, and I'll meet you back in the prison."

I shot up to where the guards were and I said, "I'm going to walk back here, and there will be one guy behind me. When he walks by, grab his tail, and throw him into one of those empty cells. Make believe he's a prisoner who's trying to escape."

A few minutes later, Spoonie came through, and the guard said, "Hey, where'd you get that uniform?"

Spoonie was hollering, "Skip, Skip!"

I just kept on walking and said, "He's not with us." After a while, I went back and got him. He was relieved to see me. Spoonie's got to be 69 or 70 now, and every time I see him we laugh about that.

I played in all kinds of places. I remember in 1949, the first year I was playing for Greenville, Alabama, and we were over in Dothan, Alabama. Our dressing room was just a dirty, filthy shed. The first night we decided we were going to shower. There were two shower heads. We were soaping up, and all of a sudden there was a snake crawling across the pipes. It emptied the place out, we never showered there again.

All the snakes weren't in the shower.

We were playing in Sioux City one year, and it was raining like crazy. The game should have been stopped. In the top of the fifth inning, we were behind 1–0, and the umpire told me, "I'm going to give you one more inning." Well in the top of the sixth, we scored nine runs, got the bases loaded with nobody out, and he called time.

We were ahead 9–1, but it reverted back to the last inning. The game was eventually called, and we got beat 1–0.

Another time I was managing in Vancouver, and we were going to Hawaii. We were playing a doubleheader in Tacoma, and we had a flight at 5:00, so there was a 4:00 time limit on the second game. We lost the first game and were getting beat in the second. I was looking at the clock. I was in the process of stalling a little bit, trying to waste time so we wouldn't play enough innings to make it an official game. I changed pitchers and had the pitcher walk guys, hit guys. Now the runners on Tacoma who made it to first were trying to get picked off, and we weren't paying any attention to them.

Anyway, I was looking at the clock out on the scoreboard, and it wasn't moving. I knew 15 minutes had passed, but the clock changed just a couple of minutes. I found out they had a kid out in the scoreboard, hanging onto the clock to keep it from going around.

Sometimes in the minors it was a real animal show. We used to play a donkey baseball game for charity at Missoula. You'd put a number of players on these two teams on donkeys, and there was always one wild-haired donkey. Big Spoonie would ride that donkey, and that son of a gun would throw him off. He'd get back on again, and it would throw him off again.

Then he'd move over to a slower donkey, but there'd be a guy going around sticking a needle in that donkey, getting the donkey to kick him off. This was long before animal rights.

One night we were sitting around in Missoula after having lost seven in a row. I suggested we have a "Break the Jinx" night. We knew this kid, Smokie, who used to sell papers on the street late at night where you could get tomorrow's newspaper. We got to be good friends with Smokie, so we dressed him up in a black outfit with a cape. I got an undertaker to bring us a hearse, and I got a gun that shot blanks. We had six of our players dressed in tuxedos like pallbearers.

It was a 7:00 game. At about a quarter to 7:00, we put a ladder along the left-field fence, and Smokie climbed up the ladder and jumped into the park.

The PA announcer yelled, "There's the jinx."

We had five or six players in our bullpen running and chasing the jinx all over the field. They brought him down around shortstop, pretended to hit him, then shot him with the blanks. So Smokie was laid out. We opened the gate and in came the hearse. We got the coffin out, and all these players walked out in tuxes. They picked up Smokie, put him in the coffin, and slid him into the hearse.

We used to go through all kinds of skits at Missoula. We had the people going crazy. The players loved it and so did the fans. We made it fun for everyone. Did it work that night with Smokie and the jinx? No, we lost again. But at least we made it entertaining.

Chapter 10

The Greatest

Jim Kaat was the first player I was around on an everyday basis whom I could tell was going to be a star. When I met him, he was just an 18-year-old kid in Missoula. He pitched 251 innings that season. It was only a 17-man roster, and we only had seven pitchers on the team. That would never happen today, the way young pitchers are babied.

Jim was one of the most fascinating young men that I ever managed. The guy had tremendous instincts, excellent knowledge of pitching, tremendous work habits, and tremendous focus.

We were a Washington Senators farm club, and Charlie Dressen was just let go as manager at Washington. He came out along with Calvin Griffith and Joe Haynes. Calvin was the president, and Joe Haynes was the vice president. Joe had pitched a number of years in the big leagues and was considered a pitching guru in the organization.

Kaat pitched a two-hit shutout, which we won 2–0. After the game, we went out to have a bite to eat. I sat down with those guys and said to Joe Haynes, "What did you think of Kaat?"

He said, "Not enough stuff to pitch in the big leagues."

I said, "I tell you what, I'll make you a bet. I'll bet you a steak dinner that within two years he pitches in the big leagues."

He said, "I'll take it."

This was 1958. In 1959, Kaat started the season at Chattanooga, and by July 1, he was leading the league in strikeouts. He was having a great year down there, so they brought him to the big leagues. He pitched his first game in Chicago on August 2.

I got on the phone to Joe Haynes and said, "Hey, where's my steak? I said two years. He made it in six months."

The guy with "not enough stuff to pitch in the big leagues" pitched 25 years in the major leagues. In today's game, if you used a radar gun, you wouldn't sign him, but he had great knowledge of pitching. He could paint the black on the inside. He could paint the black on the outside. He changed speeds.

I was his catcher as player/manager, and I saw that this guy could pitch in the big leagues. He knew how to pitch. He knew how to win.

I never did get that steak dinner, but I was just happy that Kitty got to the big leagues and was there for 283 victories. Not bad for someone with not enough stuff to make it to the big leagues.

In my mind, there is no question that more money has been wasted because of radar guns than any other reason in the history of baseball. Scouts don't scout today. Radar guns scout. And that's the problem.

As I progressed up the ladder, I had Zoilo Versalles when he was an 18-year-old kid. He eventually ended up being the Most Valuable Player in the American League in 1965. I had him in Appleton, Wisconsin. Zoilo just needed a little time to develop. He was from Cuba, and I don't think anyone ever went to the major leagues the way he did.

They called me up one day when we were in Topeka, and they said, "Get Versalles to Chicago."

Now Zoilo couldn't speak any English, and in those days air travel wasn't like it is today. So I had to put him on a train in Topeka to Kansas City. In Kansas City he had to get off the train and go to the airport to get on a plane. He was flying United to Chicago. He had to get off the plane in Chicago and go directly to the ballpark.

I didn't want him to get lost, so I got pieces of paper and I made notes. "Cab to airport in Kansas City," "United Flight No. X," "Cab from Chicago airport to Comiskey Park." I took those notes, got pins, and pinned them all to his shirt. Somehow he made it. I literally sent him to the majors.

Being from Cuba, Zoilo never liked the cold. We were in Cedar Rapids, Iowa, once early in the season, and it was cold. A guy named Burt Gunter was pitching a great game. It was a 0–0 game in the sixth inning. There was a man on third base and two outs. A nice, easy ground ball was hit to Versalles at shortstop. He picked it up, and I saw he had leather gloves on, not batting gloves—regular, fur-lined winter gloves—and he threw the ball away. So we were down 1–0.

I got pissed. I said, "Get your tail in the clubhouse." I took him out of the game. Well, I went to coach third base, and I got to thinking, "Hey, it's the sixth inning, we're freezing our butts off out here, and I sent this SOB to the clubhouse. Go get his tail out here and let him freeze with the rest of us."

He was a good kid, though, and I was so happy to see him do so well in the majors.

Tony Oliva was another great young kid, who I was lucky enough to manage in Dallas in 1963. That was with the Dallas–Ft. Worth Rangers in the Coast League. We were the only team on the road when we were at home. We used to play split doubleheaders on Sundays.

Tuesday, Friday, and Sunday we were in Ft. Worth. Monday, Wednesday, Thursday, and Sunday in Dallas. On Sunday we would play a day game in Dallas and a night game in Ft. Worth, or vice versa. Then half our games were on the road, so we were always going somewhere. On Sundays when we were home, we'd play a game and then drive 40 miles and play another game.

Tony started off very shaky. The owner of the club was named Ray Johnson, and he called Calvin Griffith, because he wanted to get rid of Oliva. "Get him out of here. He can't play. The league's too tough for him."

So Calvin called me and said, "What's the matter with Oliva?"

"Nothing," I said. "He's just in a little rut here, he'll be fine."

This was in the first three weeks of the season and he was hitting about .220. I tell Calvin, "We're going on the road for 12 days. He'll be fine. Don't worry about it."

We get on the road, and Tony goes 3-for-4, 4-for-4, and 2-for-4. His average zooms from .220 to .320. Then he started playing outstanding defense.

He was one of the three best young hitters I ever managed. The other two were Tony Gwynn and George Brett. So the end of the season came, and I was making out my scouting report on our team. I took it into the office to get it copied, and Ray Johnson says to me, "Can I have one of those?"

"Sure," I said and gave him a copy. In my report I wrote, "Tony Oliva could play in the big leagues next year."

He looked it over and said, "I've been owning Triple-A clubs and dealing with players for years, Jack. You're wrong. I want to help you,

you're making a big mistake. Oliva's not ready to play in the big leagues."

Well, I could see what was happening. Oliva was now a star. Ray Johnson wanted him back for the draw power. I said, "That's the way you feel, that's the way I feel."

I turned that report in, so be it. After the season was over, I went up to Minnesota to watch the club play. The writers up there met with me and wanted a little rundown on the prospects that I had. They asked, "Do you think Tony Oliva can play up here next year?"

"Yeah, there's only one thing that bothers me," I said.

"What's that?"

"How much above .300 he's going to hit."

You know what happened? He led the league in hitting his first two years. He hit .323 in 1964. He sure was ready to play in the big leagues. He was one of those hitters who always fouled off the "bastard pitch," and then the pitcher would throw him something he could hit.

Another special guy to me was Harmon Killebrew. I had him his last year at Kansas City in 1975. What a gem he was, class all the way. Even though he hit only .199 that season with 14 home runs, he was a gentleman all the way.

I had a lot of players who were on their way down. Guys like Dick Allen and Willie Horton. I also had a lot of young kids who were going to be future stars.

One of the smartest guys I ever managed was Cookie Rojas. Another was Garry Templeton. In San Diego I had Tony Gwynn, who was a lot like Juan Pierre. Both of those guys have tremendous dedication and want to work and be good at their trade.

Gwynn had unbelievable work habits—and not just hitting. He wanted to be a Gold Glove outfielder, so he worked every day in the outfield. He couldn't throw across this room when we first signed him, but Clyde McCullough took him out every day and had him throw from right field to stretch his arm out. And you know what? He made himself into a Gold Glove outfielder. Tony had great work habits. He's a true Hall of Famer.

Brett was another great hitter, and I was very thankful to him because when he went into the Hall of Fame on the stage in Cooperstown, he mentioned my name. He said the most important thing he learned was from his first manager, Jack McKeon, who told him to go out and relax and enjoy the game. Brett was a lot like Cookie, always thinking about what to do.

I consider it a blessing that I had two guys who had the highest batting average in the majors since 1941 when Ted Williams hit .406. Tony Gwynn batted .394 in 1994, and George Brett hit .390 in 1980. I looked it up, and Tony's is the 35th highest of all time, while George's is the 45th best mark ever. Not bad.

Robby Alomar was another guy who was always thinking. I think that Robby, of all the players I have managed in the major leagues, had the best instincts.

Joe Carter was a gamer, an intelligent player. I brought guys like Joe in to San Diego to win the pennant, and then ownership told me I made a mistake, Carter's average wasn't high enough. He hit 24 home runs and drove in 115 runs in 1990. And he was going to get better.

When they traded Joe Carter and Robby Alomar for Tony Fernandez and Fred McGriff, I almost drove off the road. Robby would have been more popular than Tony Gwynn if he stayed in San Diego. Greg Riddoch, who was the manager, kept pushing to get rid of Robby, though, because he thought he would give them trouble after they fired his father, Sandy, as coach. The kid would have been fine. And you saw what happened when those two guys went to Toronto. The Blue Jays won two World Series.

In Cincinnati I had Ken Griffey Jr. and Barry Larkin, two Hall of Famers and an up-and-coming star in Sean Casey. Casey can hit. My son, Kasey, signed Sean Casey with the Indians. The first time I met Sean in the Arizona Fall League, he was so appreciative, saying, "I owe everything to your son. He's the one who guided me. My parents love Kasey. He still stays in touch with us."

That was nice to hear. To me, Casey is almost a combination of George Brett and Tony Gwynn. That's how highly I think of him. He's a great kid, too, and during the World Series he came by just to say hi and wish me luck. I'll never forget that.

People forget that when I was managing Cincinnati, I also had Deion Sanders. I loved Deion. Deion was a very, very hard worker. He was focused. I think the football experience and how hard he had to work and prepare carried right over into baseball. He could run. I think if Deion would have devoted all his time to baseball, he would have been an All-Star. He had so much talent, but he couldn't develop all his talent because he was playing both sports. He would have become a good hitter, and I loved his personality.

Deion was the perfect guy for young ballplayers to emulate because he set the tempo. He showed them what dedication and hard work were all about. His personality was great, and he looked after the young guys. He took care of them. He made them feel comfortable. He would buy them dinner, clothes. He was a showman and a good guy.

With the Marlins, I was so lucky to have Pudge Rodriguez. He was pure gold. He's one of my all-time favorites, another Hall of Famer. Pudge bought a lot to a ballclub. He's that fiery leader type. He took a lot of pride in his work and was well-prepared every day. He did a great job handling the pitchers, and he was the guy who would give you the big RBI. Then the rest of the lineup would follow suit. I also liked that Pudge bought me cigars. He's the best catcher I've seen, and I've seen a lot of catchers.

And I saw some guys who shouldn't be catching. When I managed Triple-A Richmond in 1976, we had this young catcher, Dale Murphy. He could throw the ball 100 mph, but he couldn't get it anywhere near the base. He was such a sensitive kid that he tried too hard and wound up making it worse. They started booing him, and I sat him down to take the pressure off. When the farm director came out to see him, he was upset that I had benched his young star player. I let him have it, "Listen, you pencil-pushing SOB," I told him. "The kid's a great prospect, but he needs a break. I'll get him in when the time is right."

I finally sent him in to pinch-hit in the fourteenth inning against Memphis when we were down two runs with two men on. He homered to center, and he was a hero again. After that, he carried us the rest of the season. It was a thrill to watch him develop into the MVP he became.

Getting to be around Roger Clemens at the All-Star Game in Houston was a thrill, too. The thing about Roger is that he is always so prepared. I said to some of my players, "If you could just sit there and analyze him, emulate the way he goes about his work and notice the demeanor that he has on the mound, he never gets excited when he gets in a jam. He never gives in to the hitter. The count goes to 3–2, he doesn't rear back and try to throw harder. He's got a plan. He's a shining example of how to pitch."

During the World Series, he was so impressive to watch that I almost found myself rooting for him. But I was trying to beat him. Still, you have to admire a guy who has done it so many years.

Here's a guy who, at the time, had six Cy Young Awards and yet never lived off his reputation. And that's how he won his seventh Cy Young with the Astros. He's worked harder and harder to justify his reputation and those Cy Young Awards. That's what makes him a champion.

I've been lucky enough to have been around quite a few champions. And that's what really makes this game fun.

CHAPTER 11

Who's the Boss

Sometimes, you have to be pushy to get what you want. I had to be pushy when I was a general manager, and sometimes I have to be pushy as a manager to get what I want from my players.

Pushy is OK as long as it is done for the right reasons. That's one reason why I admire George Steinbrenner. He does what he has to do to produce a winner. He wants to win every year, but if I had my way, Yankee history would have been written a lot differently.

I picked up the nickname Trader Jack years ago because I knew how to make a deal—even before I became a GM.

We almost pulled off a great trade with the Yankees. Thurman Munson, Bobby Murcer, and Chris Chambliss were very close to being traded to the Royals when I was the manager there. It would have changed the face of the Royals and the Yankees. I really pushed for that deal, but front office interference ruined that trade. Without Munson, the Yankees wouldn't have been the same. That great Yankees-Royals rivalry of the seventies would have had some different endings, too. Cedric Tallis, the GM, didn't want to pull the trigger on the trade, though.

Cedric later went on to become the Yankees GM; he and I never really hit it off because Ewing Kauffman, the owner, hired me. I replaced Bob Lemon, who was fired after the 1972 season. I had managed in Omaha for four years and had nothing to do with Bob's firing, but some people didn't see it that way.

Once I became manager, Cedric resisted change. I knew that the Royals were a team that with a few changes could really do some damage, and I tried to make that point to Cedric. I was only trying to help Cedric. Whenever I would go up to his office to talk baseball, though, he'd pull out his putter and start putting around. I'm not a big golfer. I don't have the patience for golf, especially when I'm at the ballpark. There I am trying to talk baseball with Tallis, and he'd be saying, "Jack, I learned something the other day from my golf pro. He told me my hands were in the wrong place." His hands weren't in the wrong place, his head was. Cedric wouldn't make the deals that needed to be made.

In 1973 we were running neck and neck with Oakland. We had a chance to get right-hander Pat Dobson from the Braves for a couple kids I had at Triple-A: Norm Angelini and Al Autry. I knew these kids weren't championship players and I told Cedric to make that deal. He talked it over with the farm director Lou Gorman, and they decided they weren't about to "mortgage the future" for the present. Dobson got traded to the Yankees instead. What "mortgage the future" really means is clubs don't want to win now. Dobson even went on to beat us one game, and the writers asked me afterward if I would have liked to have Dobson on my staff. I blew up, saying, "We could have had him if we had gotten off our tails." That year we finished in second place behind the A's.

I knew we could have won the West with a few changes, but Cedric didn't want to make the moves necessary to win. He even told me, "Jack you don't have to worry about winning the pennant your first year."

Why not? When the opportunity presents itself, you win the pennant. You never know when you are going to get another chance. That's what the Marlins did in 2003 and it paid off. We made the most of that opportunity. I can never understand why you wouldn't try to win when the opportunity is there, but yet, that's the way Cedric thought.

That was too bad because Mr. Kauffman had the great idea of running a Royals baseball academy, an idea that was ahead of its time and that's how the Royals got Frank White.

That also got me in trouble with Tallis before I even became manager of the Royals. In addition to managing Omaha, I also ran the instructional league program, and Syd Thrift was doing a great job with the academy (he was a great superscout who later ran the Pirates). I had great faith in Syd's judgment. When Mr. Kauffman asked me if we had any prospects in the academy, I mentioned Frank White, Ron Washington, and a few others because Syd and I had talked about those guys. Syd knew talent and was my right-hand man. Kauffman told Tallis about this, and Tallis called me into his office. In front of Lou Gorman, Tallis said, "Jack, don't you ever lie to Mr. Kauffman again. You told him there were prospects in the academy."

Now I was really steamed and I told Tallis and Gorman there were prospects there. Gorman said his scouts didn't think so. I told them maybe they could find someone who would tell them what they wanted to hear, but this was the way I saw it. I was really high on Frank White, who went on to have a terrific career. You see, I was never Tallis' guy. I was hired by Mr. Kauffman, a good guy who was great to me.

When I became manager I had to fight Tallis to call up Frank White. Then, when they finally did let me call him up, they sent him back down even though he showed right away his value as a player. He got two hits off Jim Palmer, the Cy Young winner. Then he got three hits off Gaylord Perry and hit a line drive that almost took Nolan Ryan's head off. Our team went from third place to first, but when shortstop Fred Patek came back, White went back to the minors. Soon after, I was fired. I was replaced by Whitey Herzog. The first thing he did was put Frank White at second base. Funny how it goes.

Of course, I probably never would have gotten fired if they made the trade with the Yankees. During that World Series, we talked to the Yankees, who were interested in our big first baseman, John Mayberry, and Patek. Mayberry drove in 100 runs that year, so his market value was high.

The Yankees had just what I wanted. We needed pitching and catching. I wanted reliever Sparky Lyle, but the Yankees weren't giving him up, so I got a little creative and put together a good package. We were willing to trade Mayberry and Patek for Thurman Munson, first baseman Chris Chambliss, outfielder Bobby Murcer, shortstop Jimmy Mason, and two young minor league pitchers, Scott McGregor and Tippy Martinez.

I had seen those two pitchers at Triple A, and I knew they were going to be good. What a deal. We would have won the pennant, but Tallis didn't like it. He said, "Jack, these young pitchers, what makes you think they are going to be good?"

"Trust me, Cedric, they can pitch," I told him.

"Jack," he said, "if I make this trade, they'll run me out of town." He didn't want to trade popular players. I told him that he would own the town and that we might win the pennant in a few years if we made that trade.

Munson came back and had a great year. Chambliss had a great year, Murcer eventually went to the Giants, and the two pitchers were ready for the majors. All we would have had to give up were Patek and Mayberry. They had good years for us, but the way I look at it, you're not going to get anything good unless you give up something good.

If you're a Royals fan, you know what happened in 1976—Chambliss' home run off Mark Littell in the ninth inning of Game 5 against the Royals gave the Yankees the pennant.

No, Cedric didn't like change. At least not in baseball. He did like to change his golf grip when he got tips from his pro, though.

Yankee history also would have been a little different if I had gotten Ron Guidry when I was with the A's. That deal was set, but owner Charlie Finley squelched it. Can you imagine if Guidry had been traded before he became a Yankee star? In 1976 I managed Richmond in the International League, and Guidry was at Syracuse. I think his pitching record was 9–1. I could tell he was definitely going to be a big league star. I was managing the A's and talking with the Yankees in spring training in 1977. Charlie was hot after Dock Ellis. He eventually traded for Ellis, but he missed out on the big catch, Guidry.

He said to me, "Oh, what the hell do you know about Guidry? Just because he's 9–1 doesn't make him a big leaguer."

"Charlie," I said, "this guy can be a starter or a reliever and be an outstanding major league pitcher either way."

But Charlie didn't go for it. The season started and Guidry replaced an injured Yankees pitcher in the rotation. He won his first couple of starts, and the rest is history. He went 16–7 that year with a save, went on to win 170 games for the Yankees, and became one of the most popular pitchers ever to wear pinstripes.

Red Schoendienst, one of our coaches, had heard my conversations with Charlie. Later that year the Yankees came to Oakland, and Guidry pitched a two-hit shutout against us. Red asked me, "Jack, is that the guy you wanted?"

"Yeah, that's him," I said.

"Jack, you should be the general manager instead of manager."

We did get Dock Ellis, and he won one game and lost five for us before we traded him to Texas. If we had made that trade for Guidry, I might still be in Oakland. Maybe I should have been a little more pushy with Charlie.

Charlie did listen to me that spring when we traded Phil Garner, Tommy Helms, and Chris Batton to the Pirates. It turned out to be a pretty good deal for us because we got Dave Giusti, Doc Medich, Doug Bair, Rick Langford, Tony Armas, and Mitchell Page. Before I got involved, the Pirates wanted to give us Fernando Gonzalez, Ken Macha, Tim Jones, Odell Jones, Medich, and Giusti.

"You don't want those guys," I told Charlie.

"What do you mean, Jack?"

"Substitute," I said. "Go get Armas, go get Doug Bair and Rick Langford."

"What do you know about these guys?"

"Charlie, I just got finished managing in the International League. I know these guys. They're going to be good."

So, he went back to Pirates GM Pete Peterson. When he came back to me later in the day with the names I wanted, I said, "Now, go back and ask for one more."

"They'll think I'm crazy," he said.

"Ask for one more."

"Who should I ask for?" he asked.

"Charlie, ask for Mitchell Page, Miguel Dilone, or Ed Whitson."

"What the hell do you know about Ed Whitson. Whitson's only pitched in the Carolina League."

"Yeah, Charlie, but I managed in Puerto Rico this winter and I saw Whitson down there. He's good."

I thought they would probably give us Dilone, but they threw in Mitchell Page, and that worked out for us. That's another reason why I didn't mind managing in Puerto Rico or the minors, I got to see the young players and that really helped me later on. I eventually traded for Ed Whitson in 1982 when I was with the Padres. Whit later became a Yankee and got in that big fight with Billy Martin.

As for George Steinbrenner, I've always gotten along with him, but then again I've never had to work for him. After we won the World Series in 2003 I did get a nice letter from him. At this stage of the game I don't know if I could manage for George. I'd probably be like Don Zimmer. I'd get pissed off and tell him where to stick it.

Like I said, I'll make a deal with anyone. When my son Kasey was in college, he was having trouble in one of his classes. I was GM of the Padres and I said, "Tell the professor you'll get him tickets to the game."

"No, I can't do that, Dad," he said.

When Kasey got a "D" on his next test, he finally went to the professor and said, "Hey, anytime you need tickets to the game, I'll be glad to help you out." The guy took him up on it and pretty soon the professor was sending me cigars, and Kasey got a passing grade. That's what I call street smarts.

I finished college in 1957, but I didn't get my diploma until 1963. Back then you had to walk across the stage to get your diploma, but I was out managing every year, so I couldn't get to Elon College for the ceremony.

I knew some members of the board of directors at Elon, friends of mine in Burlington, where I managed. So I worked out a deal with them to put a little pressure on the administration to send me an absentee diploma. I was one of the first to get a diploma in the mail, along with Admiral Rickover's nephew. You can find a deal anywhere, and I always push for the best deal I can make.

I think it goes back to my cab days in South Amboy. Normal fare in the city was 75 cents. If I had a fare to the coal docks, where they unloaded the coal, I had to drive over rough terrain to get there, so I charged $1. I remember one day this guy needed to go out to the coal docks.

We got there and he asked, "How much?"

"A dollar," I said.

"I ain't paying you," he replied.

So I took a little detour of about four blocks over to city hall and pulled right up to the police station. My uncle was a captain there, so I pulled in the driveway and tooted the horn. My uncle looked out the window. "Come here a minute," I said.

He came down the steps and asked, "What's the problem?"

"I got a guy in here who won't pay."

"How much does he owe you?"

"He owes me a dollar for the cab ride and a dollar for his bull. Two bucks."

"Two bucks or 20 days," my uncle told the guy.

The guy whipped out the two bucks, and I said, "Now you can get your tail out of the cab and walk to the dock."

Whenever I made a deal as a GM, I was looking for another deal. In 1984 when we won the pennant with the Padres, we made some good deals, but I couldn't close the deal on the final piece of the puzzle I wanted. I wanted to get Dave Stewart from Texas. He was traded to Philly and then he went over to Oakland, where he became a 20-game winner four years in a row. He sure would have looked good in a Padres uniform.

Through the years I've learned that if you are looking for a pitcher, you'd better go get two in the winter. It's like developing players in a farm system. My philosophy is that you need 10 good pitching prospects to end up with two pitchers because there will be injuries, guys who can't cut it, all kinds of things.

You almost need two groups. When I was in San Diego, we had good young catchers in Mark Parent and Bob Geren. Sure, they played in the big leagues, but they never went on to blossom into what we thought they would be. We eventually wound up with Sandy Alomar Jr. and Benito Santiago as catchers.

Putting together a championship team is like putting together a big jigsaw puzzle. Back with the Padres before the 1984 season, I knew we were this close to being that kind of team. Little by little, all the pieces of the puzzle were coming together, but several key pieces had to be added through trades. I used to love to do three-way trades because even if you don't have what the other guy needs, you can find someone else who does. I still needed a lefty in the bullpen and a left fielder. The lineup was strong. We had signed Steve Garvey to play first, we moved Alan Wiggins from the outfield to play second to make room for Kevin McReynolds, who we got in the same draft as the right fielder Tony Gwynn. We traded Ozzie Smith for Garry Templeton, we signed closer Goose Gossage as a free agent, and we had solid starting pitching in Ed Whitson, Eric Show, Tim Lollar, and Mark Thurmond.

Show was a little strange, but he was a decent starter. Pat Dobson, who later became the Padres pitching coach, used to say that the Moons of Romulus had to be aligned just perfectly for everything to go right for Show on the mound. Dobber was right.

I was at the winter meetings and like always, I set up shop in the lobby. I love working the lobby. I once made a trade while I was in line to check out. On this day, I was looking for Dallas Green, the Cubs GM. The meetings were in Nashville, Tennessee, and I heard the Expos had an interest in one of my pitchers, Gary Lucas. They wanted to give me Scott Sanderson, but I didn't want to make that trade.

I did know Dallas needed a pitcher badly and I found out that he was interested in Sanderson, but he didn't have the goods to get him. Montreal didn't like anybody the Cubs were offering. I learned from my father, who used to love to trade cars, that any deal can be made, you just have to keep pushing. So I pushed.

"I can get you Sanderson," I told Dallas.

"If you get him, what do you want for him?" Dallas asked.

Now I had my opening and I took it. Remember, I wanted a left-handed pitcher and a left fielder. "How about Craig Lefferts and Carmelo Martinez?" I said. Martinez was just a rookie first baseman who could play the outfield and had played in only 28 games for the Cubs. The same went for Lefferts, he was another guy coming off his rookie year and was 3–4. The two kids were just what we needed, but not what Montreal needed. They wanted Lucas, and I had him. I went back to Montreal and told them I would make the deal if they threw in infielder Al Newman, who is now a coach with the Twins. John McHale, their GM and my old buddy, said yes. Then I went back to Dallas and made the deal—I even had him throw in third baseman Fritz Connally. I got my left fielder and my left-hander.

There was still one more piece of the puzzle we needed, an every day third baseman, someone who had postseason experience and could point the way for the young guys. That's where George came in again. That someone was Graig Nettles and he was made available by the Yankees.

It was harder to make a deal with the Yankees, though, because Steinbrenner felt I had taken advantage of him in an earlier trade when we got Ruppert Jones, Joe Lefebvre, Tim Lollar, and Chris Welsh for Jerry Mumphrey and John Pacella. He said he wasn't going to deal with me, only with club president Ballard Smith. That was OK with me. We did the trade on the phone and I sat right next to Ballard and walked him through it. On March 30, just days before the season started, we traded Dennis Rasmussen for Nettles. The puzzle was complete.

That season turned out to be a magical year for the Padres, as we won our first pennant and lost in the World Series to the Tigers. Just like after the 2003 World Series, Steinbrenner sent me a nice note. The telegram arrived after we came back from a 2–0 deficit to beat the Cubs to win the pennant. It read:

> Jack, the lion's share of the credit has to go to you. You were patient. You made some great moves. You took me to the cleaners. And I am happy for you. You should be very proud of the job you did.
>
> Sincerely,
> George Steinbrenner

Sometimes it pays to be pushy. Just ask the boss.

CHAPTER 12

Reds Storm

When I worked for the Reds as a scout and later as manager, Marge Schott, the owner, was a great cigar lover. Her husband used to smoke them. She liked the smell of them, and she liked to smoke them.

One time in spring training in Plant City, when I was managing, we went out to dinner with Jim Bowden, the general manager. Marge used to give all the club executives cars, and Jim had an SUV. He drove us to this steakhouse in Plant City. We were finishing dinner, and Marge said, "Jack, where's your cigar?"

"It's in my pocket, Marge."

"Well, you light it up, honey."

I said, "We can't do that here, these people will complain."

"The hell with them. You light it up. I just love the cigar smoke."

So I lit up, and after a few minutes, we went out to Bowden's SUV. I was going to put the cigar out and Marge said, "What are you doing?"

"I'm going to put out the cigar. Jim doesn't want smoke in the car."

She said, "This is my car, you smoke in the damn thing."

So I smoked in the damn thing.

I loved Marge, she really was a nice owner. Marge loved her dog Schotzie. It's ironic that after Schotzie II died, Marge just went like that. I think she felt all alone after losing her dog.

Marge was a straight shooter. She wasn't discreet with people around her, and that hurt her. She was herself.

I found her to be a very, very generous lady. I think through baseball, they made her look like a cheap owner—you always heard the stories about her. But deep down in her heart Marge was a very generous person. They tell me she left a lot of money to different charities, and when I was there she was always very involved in Children's Hospital functions.

She used to have this black-tie function every year in September to raise money for the Children's Hospital. She used to bring elephants out there to her place and people would ride them. I wouldn't ride any elephants. She wanted me to, but I didn't.

She had big tents at this affair. I came in and met her at the door. She said, "Where's your cigar?" I had left them in the car because I didn't think it was appropriate to smoke them at such a fancy affair.

So she took me into the kitchen, saying she had some cigars. She went into the refrigerator, whipped out these two cigars, and said, "Come on, I'll smoke them with you."

There was no telling how long she had had those cigars in the refrigerator. I mean, I know cigars, and I took the wrapper off one and bit into it, and it was like biting into a brick. Marge cranked her cigar up and I cranked up mine. I said, "I'll be right back." I ran out to my car, threw her cigar away, and grabbed two cigars.

I ran back and said, "Here Marge. Here's a fresh one."

She told me, "I always keep cigars." Yeah, she kept them all right, but there was no telling how long she kept them. Plus, she kept them in a refrigerator, not a humidor. They were half frozen.

Marge just loved to talk baseball with me around the batting cage. With her, everything was "Honey." We'd lose four or five in a row, and she'd come down and say, "Hi, honey, how's everything going?" Then she would stick this envelope in my pocket. The first time she did it, I didn't know what the hell was in there. I went back in the clubhouse to look at it, and it was dog hair, from Schotzie I. After Schotzie I died, she shaved off all his hair and saved it for good luck. So after that we were going along pretty well, but then we lost two or three in a row, and she came again with another packet of Schotzie's hair.

I had more hair in my office than they had in a dog pound.

One day she couldn't come down to the field for some reason. So she called me in my office about 15 or 20 minutes before the game. She said, "Hi, honey. Sorry Schotzie and I couldn't make it down to the field today, but we were thinking about you. And Schotzie wants to say something to you."

And then she said, "Bow wow" over the phone. "Schotzie wants to say bow wow and good luck."

I said, "OK."

In the past, I had some players who were dogs, but this was the first time I ever had a conversation with a dog. A lot of managers might not want to put up with something like that, but Marge always meant well. She cared about her team and her dogs. They were the two great loves of her life.

I first met Marge when I was managing the Padres. Joan Kroc introduced me to her. Then after I was let go by the Padres, I went home and laid low for awhile. About the second of January in 1993, Jim Bowden called me. I had met the guy one time before through my old friend Syd Thrift.

Jim called and said, "Hey, I'm looking for an experienced guy, I want somebody to do some scouting in Arizona. Would you be interested?"

I said, "I don't know, let me think about it."

I took about five days before I called back. It was a good chance to get out, so I took the job for $5,000 plus expenses. Evidently, he liked what I was doing. He kept calling and wanted me to go to work full-time as a major league scout.

I said, "Let me think about it."

He kept calling, and I kept saying, "Let me think about it."

Finally, Carol said, "Do you want to work or don't you? Why do you keep telling the guy to call back?"

I said OK and went to work for him. They gave me some title like "senior advisor for player personnel." I scouted for a couple of years, and one day Bowden asked me, "You'd like to manage again, wouldn't you?"

I said, "Yeah," and that was the end of it. All of a sudden they fired Tony Perez and hired Davey Johnson. Marge was very close with Ray Knight and had insisted that he be the bench coach and manager-in-waiting. They fired Davey and gave Ray Knight the job. He stayed on a year and a half, and then they fired him. Bowden called me one day near the end of July 1997 while I was scouting in El Paso. He said, "What are you going to do?"

"I'm going over to Phoenix to watch the Giants."

He said, "Just come on in here, you don't need to see them."

I flew to Cincinnati. I was there one night and Jim said to me, "We're going to make a change. We want you to manage. Just be over here at 10:00 in the morning."

I hadn't brought any clothes. I didn't have anything with me, I had no idea I was going to manage the club. So I took over, and our first trip was to San Diego. I went down to my guy at Brady's Men Shop and ended up buying myself some new clothes. I got the job and I got the new clothes. Not a bad deal.

When I took over that club, Bowden told me, "This club can't win." I said, "That's a bunch of crap. We're going to win."

I had 63 games, and we were 33–30. Then they hired me again, then hired me again, then hired me again. My second full season there, we were 96–67. That was my 50th year in professional baseball, and I was named Manager of the Year. We lost a one-game playoff to the Mets for the wild-card, and that kept us out of the postseason. But I was proud of that team.

There were a lot of players on that team I loved. Sean Casey said one of the nicest things I've ever heard said about me. He said, "When I felt no one else in the park was on my side, I always knew Jack was. Jack would let us make our mistakes and just put us out there again the next time."

Pokey Reese was another one of those guys. Pokey was a great kid. He was a utility guy when I took over the club, but I had seen him play when he was in the minor leagues. They had Barry Larkin at shortstop, Bret Boone at second, and I started putting Pokey at third base for defense. This guy was a Gold Glove at second, short, and third, in my opinion. I started to put him at third base, and we started to take off. He played third base like Brooks Robinson, and he started hitting a little bit. He was my regular third baseman the rest of the year. In the winter, we traded Bret Boone. Bowden was saying, "We've got to get a second baseman," and they were throwing all these names out there.

I said, "Don't worry about it. I've got the guy. This guy can play second, he can play short, he can play third." They didn't have as much faith in Pokey as I did. But I got Pokey at second where he won a Gold Glove. Pokey was like Bip Roberts in San Diego. He could play anywhere; he could bunt; he was receptive to instruction; and you just had to get him to be the hitter he was, a singles or doubles hitter. You didn't try to get him to hit the ball out of the ballpark. To this day, when I see Bip, he says, "Jack's my daddy, he took care of me." It was the same way with Pokey. You need players like that to be a winning team.

I got along with Jim Bowden fine. There were some great people with the Reds. Hall of Fame writer Hal McCoy and Hall of Fame broadcaster Marty Brennaman were two of my favorites of all time. We had a lot of fun, it was a great bunch.

I'm my own man, and sometimes that's not good. But I just have to be me. What you see is what you get. If you don't want it, then don't hire me.

After I was named Manager of the Year in 1999, they didn't want to give me anything. I could see the handwriting on the wall. And there were some deals over there I didn't like.

I didn't want to trade Mike Cameron for Ken Griffey Jr. Cameron was another young guy I gave a chance to, and he took advantage of that opportunity. That really helped the chemistry of the team. The same went for Pokey Reese and Sean Casey. All three were great kids. Bowden wanted Griffey in the worst way, and he got him before the 2000 season. I can understand what he was trying to do.

Griffey is a great ballplayer. He hit 40 homers that first year, but because of injuries, it really hasn't worked out the way people thought it would for him in Cincinnati. All I can say about that is that we had a good ballclub before he got there, and ever since he got there it hasn't worked out. It's too bad he's been injured so much.

That's the thing about this game. It's not always about the talent, but how that talent fits together on a team and how the injuries affect the team. We finished in second place in 2000 with an 85–77 record. That was my last year there. The Reds haven't come close to finishing .500 since.

But I'm a much better manager today because of my Cincinnati experience. That last year, some players crapped all over me. They weren't going to do that to me in Florida. I learned something right there that got me to where I am today. I had to deal with some difficult situations in Cincinnati. Some players had a lot of freedom. In Cincinnati I didn't have the support, as far as players going up to the front office and griping and wanting something done.

In Florida they don't do that.

I always tell management, especially with teams that have struggled before I took over: "Do you want to win here?"

They say, "Yeah."

I say, "If you want me to do it your way, I'll be glad to do it your way and finish down at the bottom. Or would you rather win?"

They say, "We want to win."

And I say, "Well then, let me do it my way."

These days you have to push the players, you can't let the players push you around. We are not a babysitting service. Major League pitchers should be ready to pitch. If you can't use some of these relievers two or three days in a row, maybe they need to expand the rosters so you can carry 15 pitchers.

If you want to win, you've got to use your best.

Don Gullett was the pitching coach with me when I was with the Reds, and he is one of the best. We were talking about the year that we won 96 games. We had to use Scott Sullivan, Scott Williamson, and Danny Graves every day.

You don't want to bring in some donkey, you want to bring in the guys you are going to win with. You bring in your best, maybe win the game, and maybe tomorrow you don't have to use him. My philosophy has always been that you win the game today, the heck with tomorrow. I'm interested in winning today, I don't care about what's going to happen tomorrow or the next day.

Win today, it may rain tomorrow.

Even if you do win, you still get criticized by all these *Moneyball* guys, who love to run around screaming, "Burnout, burnout."

You get one guy who gets an injury, and it's because it's how you used him. Heck, you can get hurt anytime. Johnny Sain's theory was that players have fewer injuries when active than they do when they are inactive. That's a great theory. Johnny Sain was my pitching coach at Richmond with the Braves organization in 1976. The Braves have been using that philosophy all these years and they rarely have guys with bad arms.

When I left the Reds, I had nothing to be ashamed of. I did my job and worked with some great people. But I did feel unfulfilled. I felt I was going to get one more chance. I never lost hope. I just didn't know it was going to take nearly three years to get that chance.

My turning around the Reds gave the Marlins the idea to hire me. They wanted a manager who could turn the team around in the middle of a season.

Everything worked out for the best. Except for the Reds.

CHAPTER 13

Kidding Around

Good team chemistry is a must. The guys have to like being around one another, even if they get into a little mischief. Sometimes you have to look the other way when guys are looking for trouble.

The key to managing young players is you just have to find a way to communicate with them. Even when they don't speak English. It's like when I was managing in Missoula in the late fifties and we had a number of Cuban players. Because of the language barrier, we had a little problem with our signs, but I fixed that. One day I bought some big index cards. In Spanish, I wrote all the key phrases on the index cards: hit and run, bunt and steal, etc. I took them with me to third base. There was no way they were going to miss these signs. And it worked, it just took some creativity.

Sometimes, words aren't enough. In Wilson, North Carolina, I had a Cuban player named Juan Visteur. Juan was a good center fielder, but a terrible base runner. He never wanted to stop at third base. I'd have my hands up and be yelling, "Whoa, whoa," but this horse would keep on going right through my stop sign and he'd be out by 15 feet. I was fed up. I was going to fix him. I told Juan, "You do that again and I'll shoot you."

I wasn't kidding. I had picked up a couple blank guns in Greensboro and was going to put them to good use with Juan. I stuck the guns in my back pocket and went out to coach third. Sure enough, it wasn't long before Juan ran right through my stop sign, he had been on second base. The second baseman had knocked down the ball and Juan thought it was in the outfield. I put my hands up and shouted, "Whoa, whoa." Juan must have thought I was saying, "Go, go," and off he went. Right past me. So I did what I told him I was going to do: I shot him.

I reached for my guns and "Pow! Pow!" It was like Saturday afternoon at the movies. I must have fired seven or eight shots, and Juan heard them all. About 30 feet from home he ducked for cover. As it turned out, they threw the ball away and he would have been safe, but he wouldn't move. He was scared to death. He thought he was shot. After that, I never had a problem again with him running through my stop sign. Like I said, you just have to be creative.

That's the way it was in the minor leagues. You could make your point, have some fun, and move on. If I pulled a trick like that today I'd be in big trouble.

Another time in Missoula, I had this 18-year-old Cuban player named Sandy Valdespino. He was 5'8", 170 pounds. He went on to play seven years in the majors. Sandy roomed with Jim Kaat. Jim was 6'4". Mutt 'n' Jeff. Whenever they would go out to eat, Sandy would order whatever Jim was getting. A lot of the Latin players did that because they had trouble with the language. Jim and Sandy's favorite meal was ham and eggs, so naturally we nicknamed them Ham and Eggs. Well, Eggs thought he was a lot faster than he was, and that got him in trouble with me. His first game, the score was tied, and Sandy led off the ninth inning with a triple. In this situation you want to play it safe. There were no outs, so I told him, "Sandy, wait until the ball goes through the infield before you run, *comprende?*" Sandy nodded yes and said, "*Sí.*"

I thought he understood, but he really didn't. On the first pitch, batter Jay Ward hit a chopper down to third. I was following the ball, then I looked to third and there was no Sandy. He was gone. He took off for home and was out by 10 feet. We lost the game in 10 innings.

But that was just the start of it. The next night we were in another tie game, and Sandy led off the ninth with a single. The move was to sacrifice him to second. My number two hitter, Benny Sinquefield, did his job and put down a perfect sacrifice bunt to the pitcher. The only play was to first, but there went Sandy like a bat out of hell. He didn't stop at second, no he wanted to be greedy and take third, too. The pitcher turned and threw the ball. Sandy was out by 15 feet. I was fuming.

This time, I went to the hardware store and bought a clothesline. My first base coach was Gene Curtis, and I said to him, "The next time that little SOB gets to first base, I want you to lasso him."

Gene looked at me like I was crazy, but sure enough, Sandy walked and I sent the batboy out to first base with the clothesline. Curtis tied it around Sandy, whose eyes got so big, I thought they were going to pop out of his head. But I made my point. We never had a problem with Sandy again.

With the Marlins, I'm old enough to be these kids' grandfather, but it doesn't matter, I can still relate to them. I never have a problem dealing with young players.

This last spring training I was fortunate to have two players in camp whose fathers I happened to manage. I managed Bob Oliver and his son Darren and John Wathan and his son Derek. Not many managers can say that. I guess when something like that happens, you could say you're getting old. The way I'm going, I may manage somebody's grandkid before I'm done.

I'm not getting old, but they are.

The secret to dealing with young people in any business is to show them you care. The younger guys are looking for some attention. They are looking for someone who cares. You've got to show them you care about them.

Players can be very insecure. I know that sounds crazy, but it's true. You have to keep putting them out there until they realize you have faith in them. You try to help them in their baseball life but also in life. You try to educate them. Hell, I've got 50 years of experience here. I've seen every situation that could develop. One of the big problems with our country is we put too many of our seasoned citizens out to pasture, we don't use their knowledge and experience.

I try to tell these kids to stay in a straight line, stay away from this and that. You have to give them tough love. If you get on their tails, you have to turn around the next day and pat them on the back. I did that with the big boys on the pitching staff, Josh Beckett and Brad Penny.

I told them, "Look, if I didn't like you, I wouldn't get on your tail. But you've got so much ability, and I don't give a crap if you like me or you if you don't like me, I'm going to make you a 20-game winner. And I'm going to stay on your tail until you get it right."

And you know what happens? At the end of the year they're all getting it right. Josh Beckett has some great years ahead of him.

A kid like Dontrelle Willis is a joy to be around. I told him the game hasn't changed since I started playing in 1949. It's all about throwing strikes. Make 'em hit the ball and put it in play. That's when he is at his best.

We went out and won a World Championship when no one gave us a chance. It was because our young guys developed. They matured quicker than anyone thought they would. It's a little easier to mature when you have someone with 50 years of experience around them, someone who can tell them what's going on.

This game is always a challenge. Sure, we won the World Series, but as soon as we got together for spring training the next season, I had to get on them again. I told them what we did last year was history. The record books are full of one-year phenoms. We want consistency.

Sometimes they forget and they have to be reminded. I tell them, "Hey, how'd you make out last year doing what I wanted you to do? And you did it. I'm so proud that you listened, but you deserve the credit because you did it on your own. Now continue. Don't let up, because now you've got to go a little bit higher. Let's not rest on our laurels and think we have it made."

This isn't rocket science, but it is dealing with people, and in a lot of ways, that's a lost art these days because everything is done on a computer, everything is numbers. People forget there are actual people involved here, and you have to talk to them, especially the young guys. You have to mold them.

Take, for instance, a guy like Mike Lowell. He's a veteran. I don't have to talk to Lowell every day. I don't have to motivate him. I don't have to smoke him, because he does everything right. Jeff Conine is another one. I leave those guys alone. They are professionals. Let them do the job and stay out of the way. One day I may say to Mike, "How's it going." Then, three days from now, I may talk to him again for three minutes.

It's the young guys who are the challenge because they have unbelievable ability and don't know how to get it done, or they don't want to work that hard, or—and this happens all the time—no one has ever told them how to get it done.

That's exactly what happened when I took over this team. These young guys, they were like jewels, they had the ability but nobody ever pushed them. It's like being a parent. Too many parents want to be friends with their kids instead of being parents.

We had great ability here. They came into the big leagues and this is the way it was. They followed the lead of everyone else. If you didn't want to do any work, you didn't do any work and no one said anything.

Then I came along and said, "Hey, that ain't going to work boys. We've got to get our work in every day. You've got too much ability to not have consistent success. You are not applying yourself, you are not focusing, you are not working hard enough. You want something in this life, you've got to work at it."

And you know what, they all started to work. And it paid off in a World Championship, beating the Yankees at Yankee Stadium.

That's something these guys will have for the rest of their lives. It's like Beckett said to one of the writers about me, "Jack finds everybody's little niche."

Josh said he needed a little pressure, and other guys play better when they're relaxed. He said, "Jack has just has his way about him. He's got some good people skills."

That's something I learned over time. Like any parent, you have to keep after it. Just because you won a World Championship doesn't mean it's going to be easy the next season. Just because your company is on top one year, doesn't mean it's going to be on top the next season or even the next quarter.

That's why as soon as we got together for spring training, I brought my starting pitchers together and said, "Look, I'll tell you one thing, boys, you guys are the leaders. Everybody on that field is looking up to you.

"You are the World Champions. I want to see you guys set the example this year. You knew what it took to get here. You knew what it took to win the World Series, now don't slack off in your duties. I want a businesslike approach. I put each of you in a group as a leader of that group. No one screws around. If anyone on that field screws around, you jump on them, you take charge. You show them this ain't the way we do it.

"I want you to be the first one on the field running, the first one doing the fundamentals. I want everything done the correct way, and you guys are going to set the tone!"

I then met with the entire team. When I finished talking, Brad Penny got right up and said, "All right guys let's go. Let's go to work."

Everybody looked at him, like hey, we better work. Then he goes around and puts a *C* on his shirt like *Captain*. I have fun with it and I start calling him Captain. He's really a good guy, he was just never challenged before I got here. And giving him authority, I helped him grow stronger, I never had to worry about his work habits.

It's like our closer in 2004, Armando Benitez. All I heard was how he was going to be a problem. But he was great from the start. I just kept preaching to him, "Hey, you have good stuff, you don't have to try to overthrow. You'll throw just as hard by not overthrowing." And now his stuff is sinking. That's what happens when you relax.

He's worked hard. From the start of spring training he was at the ballpark an hour or two before the rest of the guys. He worked out in the weight room and on the bike—that's how he got into shape. Armando wound up with a team record 47 saves for us. Killing 'em with a little love goes a long way. That's what it is all about.

You have to go with the flow a bit, too. One day last season we had a "bring your dog to the game" promotion. Instead of getting upset by it, I played along and had a great time. We brought in Father Joe Spina to bless the dogs. We were in a little batting slump at the time, so I said to him, "While you are here Father, how about blessing our bats, too."

It worked, we beat the Astros 6–2, and Mike Lowell hit two home runs.

I look at myself as a salesman. A big part of that is telling the truth to the players and letting them know you trust them. Be honest with them. These guys can't pull anything on me, I've seen it all and done a lot of it.

I just show them a little trust. Too many people in charge are afraid to do that. They'll come up to me in spring training and say, "Skip, can I drive up here with my family?" Sometimes I let them. That shows them a little respect. Twenty years ago, I probably wouldn't have done that. I might have been trying to get an identity as a big league manager and probably would have said, "No, one rule for everybody."

You've got to have certain rules for everybody, but somewhere along the line you have to have some leeway. You've got to almost take each situation for what it is worth. In different situations, different things come up—that's what managing people is all about. Use your age and your experience to your advantage.

I like to let the players use their imagination. I don't want robots. I don't want guys who need to be told what to do. There is no way they are going to expand their baseball knowledge if you're going to call every pitch, call every play. Somewhere along the line they have to figure out things for themselves. The same goes for business. Let them grow.

Another thing with young kids is sometimes you want them to get beat up a little bit. It shows them they still have a lot to learn and then when you send them out the next time, they'll work that much harder. It's how they learn.

CHAPTER 14

Mind Games

There's the Harvard Business School and there's the McKeon Business School. Here's how mine works. I've seen so many guys in baseball try to push themselves into a job, and that's how they blow the job.

They become victims of the country club syndrome, you know, push everybody else out of the way so they can get to the top. But you never get there, because you've alienated too many people along the way. I don't do it that way. I just tell them what I know and let it go. If they like me, fine, if not, I can always go back to the Y and play on that softball team.

Another problem with pushing too hard for a job is that if you advertise too much, you dig your own grave. Here's what happens if you're going for a job and everybody knows it—and this is true across the board from baseball to the boardroom—if you push yourself too much, sooner or later, your enemies are going to find out you want the job; when they do, they will shoot you down before you even get a foot in the door.

There is the right time and the wrong time to be pushy. When you are going for a job, you can't come on too strong. There's a ladder to success and a back door to success. Whenever possible, try to take the back door. Your enemies may not even know you, but they may want the job or be linked to someone who wants the job. The more people who know you are seeking the position, the less chance you have of getting it.

For example, if the Dodgers managing job were open and I announced my interest in it, the people in that organization who don't like me are going to tell Dodgers owner Frank McCourt, "Hey, stay away from that guy." And he will. That's human nature.

Always keep your job searches low key. I've told a lot of my friends that, but they still don't listen.

Before I had any real clout in the majors as a GM, I had to get in the World Series in 1984. After that I had credibility and was able to make more moves. Winning my first Manager of the Year Award gave me credibility as a manager. It took a few years for that to pay off, but when it did, I landed a great job.

You can't force yourself on people. If you give good advice, they'll come around. It works with any business. It works for teams, too. All through the 2003 season, we took everything in stride. We didn't put any extra pressure on our guys, saying we had to win this series or that series. And that is the same way I operated in 2004. I told the guys, "This is a continuation of last season. Just keep playing the way you did."

There is a difference between forcing yourself on people and being persistent.

Padres owner Ray Kroc, the man who created the McDonald's empire, taught me that. Ray was 52 when he met the McDonald brothers and started over in a new field, handling the franchising of the restaurants, and he built that business into a fortune. Ray ran the Padres until he died in 1984, when his wife Joan took over the club.

Look at my career. I couldn't hit. I couldn't play. I'd get going as a manager and then I'd get released and start over. But I kept being persistent. I kept following my dream, being persistent without being pushy. I kept making contacts, trying to sell myself and eventually I did.

When I got fired as manager of the Kansas City Royals, I went down and managed in Triple A. You have to take any route you can to get back. Yeah, I swallowed my pride and went back to the minor leagues after being a big-time major league manager, but it was something I had to do to get back. The problem is a lot of guys today won't swallow their pride. That's why I think it is interesting what Bobby Valentine is doing, managing in Japan after being let go by the Mets.

I swallowed my pride and went back to Richmond. Then I came back to manage the A's, got fired there, swallowed my pride again and went back to manage Denver in Triple A. Before I knew it, I was general manager of the Padres. And I made that time in the minor leagues pay off by studying other teams' young players who I could grab later in trades. Every time I met with adversity, it worked out to my advantage. But I stayed persistent. I had a goal in mind and I never let it go.

I also was smart with my money. That gave me some freedom. Baseball numbers aren't the only numbers I like to play around with. I like the stock market, too.

My first year managing in the big leagues I was paid $30,000 by the Royals. I didn't give a darn about the money. I was interested in proving I could do the job. We finished second behind the A's, and they had a good team. At the end, we went into Oakland for a four-game series and we lost three out of four. Catfish Hunter shut us out, Vida Blue shut us out. The season's over and we had a young pitcher named Doug Bird. I think the minimum was $16,000. Cedric Tallis, the general manager, said to me, "Imagine that son of a gun, he wants $40,000." We only brought him up in the middle of the season and he wanted $40,000, but I didn't think anything of it. A week later Cedric told me, "Yeah, I finally got Bird to agree at $32,500." When the season ended, Cedric told me, "I can get you a little raise. I can pay you $32,000."

He was paying this rookie $32,500 and was only going to give me $32,000 after we finished second and were in the race until the last series of the year. So I grabbed him and said, "Let me tell you one thing, if you don't think I'll tell you to stick this job where the sun doesn't shine, than you're like to see it." Out the door I went.

I drove home to North Carolina. By the time I got home, Carol said, "Cedric's called five times. He wants you to call him."

I waited another day, and then I finally called him. Cedric told me that Ewing Kauffman wanted me back. So I flew back out to Kansas City and went to Mr. Kauffman's office. It was a bad financial year with the recession and all. So he said to me, "Jack, I'd like to pay you more money, but I'm really strapped."

I listened to that sob story until he said, "I can give you $35,000." I was only looking for $40,000 really, so I took $35,000. I was happy. At Christmastime I got a nice letter from Mr. Kauffman, thanking me for my hard work and loyalty to the organization. As a personal gift he gave me 100 shares of his company, Marion Labs, and 200 shares of King Radio. Marion Labs was worth $40 a share, so there was $4,000. And King was worth about $10 a share, so there was $2,000, for a total of $6,000. It all came to $41,000, better than where I thought I would be.

But I didn't stop there. I kept that 100 shares of Marion Lab, and it eventually went to $50 a share. The next year I went out and bought 100 shares at $5,000. I broke it up into 50 shares apiece for my four kids and let it sit. In 13 years it had split eight times, and the last time I figured it out, each one of those kids had $74,000. They started buying houses and stuff, sold their stock, and then the company merged. I ended up selling King Radio at $20 a share. So no, I didn't get the raise I wanted, but the truth is, I did a hell of a lot better. In the end, I made over $300,000 on that deal.

That's what I mean about being smart. Even when I was sitting home for two years before the Marlins called, I never gave up hope that I would manage again. I had confidence in myself and I made a lot of friends in the game. A lot of people respected me. Bill Beck is one of those guys. He was persistent in backing me. He consistently said he had the right guy to manage this team. To me, he's got to be the MVP of all this.

It was just a case of waiting to see what happened and hoping that someone would have the courage to turn back the clock and hire a 70-year-old guy. And Mr. Loria did that.

It's no big deal now. They are doing it in other sports with Hubie Brown and Joe Gibbs. Coaches and managers like us, we've made all the mistakes. We've already made as many mistakes as can be made, and we've learned from them. A new guy hasn't made half the mistakes and still has a lot to learn.

We are going to be able to get the job done quicker because of the wisdom we have. I've established a lot of new territory for these 60-plus-year-old guys, and not just in sports, but in business, too. And I'm proud of that.

I do a lot of talks for companies, and now executives are telling me they're looking for the older person to hire. That's what I want to hear.

There's also another plus in hiring someone like me. We're not in it just for the money. We're in it for the love of the game. I enjoy what

I'm doing, I absolutely love it. Am I going to let money stand in the way of doing the job I love? No.

I saw Tommy Lasorda recently and I told him, "Tommy, you oughta come back and manage somewhere." Down the road he might. That would be fun.

Everybody thinks the older guy has trouble relating to the kids, but it's the kids who love us. Hell, kids always get along better with their grandfathers than they do with their fathers, anyway. They respect us. Every once in awhile I hear a player say something about me or I read it in the paper, something like, "Hey, Jack has been around so long we've got to learn something from him." They are taking advantage of my experience, thinking I am going to help them in some way. I love the fact that Joe Paterno is still coaching. We are proving the point that experience should not be thrown out the window. It's good to have us old goats around. Look at Joe Torre, before he got the job with the Yankees, some people thought he would never win. But all that experience Joe gained over the years helped him.

I'm even the motivator for the NHL San Jose Sharks. We were in Denver where the Sharks were playing, and their general manager wanted to have breakfast with me. He wanted to know what to tell his players and what I told the guys in Game 6 to motivate them. I told them to go out and have fun, that the pressure was on Colorado. San Jose won that night. After that, their manager was calling every day.

I've worked for a lot of owners, but Jeffrey Loria is the best. He cares about his people. He even gave me a beautiful Mercedes to show how much he appreciated the job I did. Jeffrey is just a very generous person. So, after all those years in baseball, this turned out to be the best situation for me.

Here's another tip from the McKeon Business School. When you are negotiating a contract in any business, you should always ask for more than you expect to get. Don't be bashful. Ask for $25,000 extra. You might not get the 25K, but you may get 15K, 10K, or 5K more. Don't be afraid to bluff.

Baseball is full of mind games. It's been that way forever. I remember managing against my old friend Chuck Weatherspoon one day in 1969. I was in Omaha, Spoonie was in Denver. It was the first time we had been opponents, and I wanted to break his concentration at the plate. He got up there and dug in really good, like he always did. It was my chance. He must have dug a four-inch hole with his spikes. There was a rake in our dugout. I grabbed it and tossed it out onto the field. "Weatherspoon," I yelled, "As long as you're gardening, why don't you use this?" It worked. Spoonie lost his concentration and struck out on three pitches.

That's why I try to keep my players relaxed. You can't play this game tense. There's all different ways to keep your team loose. Once in the minors, when the Beatles were the big thing, I went to exchange lineup cards wearing a Beatles wig. The ump didn't like it. He wanted to throw me out before the game even started. I told him, "You can't do that. And you can't tell me how to wear my hair."

Look at the Red Sox and all the fun they had winning the World Series in 2004. Everybody was worried about their long hair. They should have been worried about how they could hit and pitch. For three straight years, wild-card teams have won the World Series. Those teams were more relaxed, thinking they had nothing to lose.

When I wore that wig, the players got a big kick out of it. We were really struggling at the time. This was in Atlanta in 1964. We had all kinds of problems at the start, guys with the German measles, for example, and we got off to a terrible 0–9 start.

So, one day I went to the novelty store and loaded up. Besides the wig, I got a plastic golf club, just in case the umps were calling low strikes, I'd break the club out. They did, and I tossed the club on the field. Everybody got a laugh out of that.

There's a saying in baseball: when the hitter is ahead in the count, you give the green light if you want him to swing and not take the next pitch. Of course you don't show him a real green light, there's just a sign for it—unless you're me.

I picked up one of those lights that light up when you touch them against metal. I painted it green, and when the time called for it, I gave my players the green light. Another time I painted a flashlight green. They loved it. It broke up the monotony of the season. That's really what you are trying to do, keep it fresh, keep your team relaxed.

At Omaha in 1971 I even had fun with the team's broadcaster Mark Holtz. His wife picked us up at the airport after one trip and she was complaining that the front wheels were making a funny noise. The next time we went on a trip, the night before, I took a screwdriver, popped off the hubcap on the front tire, and put some rocks in there. She drove us to the airport the next day and the tire is going, bing-bong, just an awful noise, and she told Mark, "I told you to get this fixed."

Sometimes a player can be a little too relaxed. You can get some real characters in this game, especially in the minors. One of the all-timers was this guy named Bill Faul. This was in Omaha, 1969, my first year managing in the Kansas City organization. It was an expansion team, so the Triple A club was stocked with veterans on the way down. Faul was a pitcher who started with the Tigers in 1962 and had something like a 12–16 major league record. He was hoping to hook on to a major league club one last time, and that's why he was with us.

One night we were in Des Moines, and the clubhouse runway was flooded. One of the guys found a frog and ran it down to the bullpen, saying Faul was going to eat it for $50. Faul got one of the guys to wash off the frog, give him a cup of water, and sure enough, he ate the thing. All that was left was the bones he spit out. Bill Faul made his 50 bucks.

This guy would eat anything. We didn't have to take him to a restaurant, just to a pet store. To be honest, I didn't like it one bit. One day in Indianapolis, Faul had made a bet he would eat a parakeet. He picked out this blue parakeet in a pet store, and the nice lady behind the counter asked, "Would you care for some bird food?"

"No," Faul said, "it ain't going to live that long."

That night between the doubleheader games he bit the bird's head off. It was gross, but that's the kind of character you run into in the minor leagues.

I loved my time in Omaha. We won the pennant in 1969 and 1970, and I had some great guys like Fran Healy down there. Fran was a catcher for nine years in the majors and has been a broadcaster for the Mets the last 21 years.

Those players were a goofy bunch, and part of being a manager to a group like that is you have to let them have their fun. You just have to make sure it doesn't get too out of hand.

One day our bus was late leaving the hotel. It was raining and most of my guys were standing under the canopy at the hotel, waiting for the bus and watching the rain. Some lady backed up into a city bus. It was just a fender bender, and the city bus driver came out to talk to her. In the meantime, one of my players, Dennis Paepke, a catcher-outfielder, walked onto the city bus and told all the passengers to get off. He told them another bus was coming. "C'mon, everybody off," he shouted, and they listened. Everybody piled off the bus and stood there in the rain as Paepke walked back under the canopy and watched them all get soaked.

In 1970 we played the Syracuse Chiefs in the Junior World Series. Bobby Cox was their third baseman. We lost, but flying back to Omaha, we had an early-morning layover in Chicago. The airport restaurant was just preparing to open, so Paepke, Healy, and I walked into the kitchen. The kitchen help didn't know who we were, and we started going around, touching different things, checking for dust and dirt, telling them we were with the health department. We got ourselves some plates and asked if we could sample the food. We piled up a huge plate of bacon, another with eggs and took them out to the rest of the team.

We didn't win the Junior World Series, but we did get a free breakfast.

CHAPTER 15

Say Again

I have a problem learning names. Like when we traded for Cubs first baseman Hee-Seop Choi before the 2004 season. We couldn't afford to keep Derrek Lee. It was tough to lose Lee, but I wasn't going to sulk.

In spring training, I started calling Choi "I-Hop." He liked that. I'm always mixing up names. That way, when I do make a mistake, people don't know if I'm kidding or not. I call our left fielder Jeff Conine "Ted," and he calls me "Steve." I don't think we ever call each other by our real names.

When I go into that clubhouse, I'm not afraid to make fun of myself. I guess there is a little Casey Stengel in me. I mispronounce a word or call someone by a wrong name. It keeps things loose. It keeps the players guessing.

People didn't think Casey knew what he was doing, either, when the Yankees first hired him as manager. I loved Casey, and I used to sit with him in the lobby during winter meetings. Like Danny Murtaugh, my mentor with Pittsburgh, Casey was a great double-talker.

We'd just sit there and talk. Casey liked to tell stories and liked the stage; we're both good actors. He was a very, very funny guy.

You'd be talking about some outfielder, then all of a sudden in the middle of the conversation Casey would just drop in some double-talk—maybe something about lunch, saying, "That pastrami sandwich I had at the deli was terrific."

"Say what, Casey?"

Then, before you know it, all of a sudden you'd start thinking about what you had for lunch. Then Casey would switch gears again, and he'd be talking about that outfielder again.

I think that's how he kept ahead of some people. Casey was always ahead of the game. Just as his mind was always going in two different directions, he's the one who came up with the idea of platooning players. Batting a left-handed hitter against a right-handed pitcher and batting a right-handed hitter against a left-handed pitcher.

Casey changed the game. I remember once hearing Mickey Mantle saying his father knew that someday there would be platooning in baseball, so that's why he taught him how to switch-hit. This was back in the thirties.

Casey would ramble on and on, but he was a baseball genius. Besides platooning players, Casey was ahead of his time in another way, too, in how he used his bullpen. He used his whole roster, and it really paid off.

In that way, Casey and I are alike, too. I like to use my entire roster. We also thanked our players the same way. When Casey won his first championship, he said the same thing I did, "I want to thank all these players for giving me the thrill of my life."

I knew exactly what Casey was talking about after we won the World Series. That's exactly how I felt, too. After 50-some years in the game, they made it possible for me to win a championship. My players gave me the thrill of a lifetime.

And just like when Casey messed up names, they thought I didn't know their names. When I do mess up a name, I know the players are sitting around smiling, thinking, "That SOB forgot my name again."

It's like dealing with the media. Too many managers don't want to work with the media. I like to have fun with the media, just like Casey did. Down at the All-Star Game in Houston, a couple of writers came up to me and said, "Jack, you'd be a hit in New York."

I guess I would have fun in New York because I would always give the writers something to write about. That's part of the game, too. I give them a quote or I give them a laugh. In Cincinnati when we had a lot of injuries and somebody asked me about RBIs one day, I said, "Shoot, we have more MRIs than RBIs."

The media is part of the game, and I like working with them. Through the years, I've talked to a lot of reporters, and I find it to be one of the best parts of the job.

It's like my writers in Florida. They're a good bunch of guys. Every day during the season, we sit in my office for a little while and talk. "What you got for me today, guys?" I always ask. The writers are the link to the fans so it's important to let them know how you feel about things, even if it means sometimes you get upset. I understand they have a job to do, and nobody really knows how hard they work, either. They come to the ballpark almost as early as I do and they are the last to leave by the time they are done with their stories. They're away from their families just like the players and staff. It's not easy.

When I became a GM, it was the same way. I talked to the writers every day. After the 1979 season in Denver, I was burned out from managing, so San Diego was the perfect spot to land. After being an assistant GM for a year, I became vice president of baseball operations. And that is where I earned the nickname "Trader Jack."

I knew how to get a deal done. Whenever I was in the owner's box and Ray Kroc wasn't there, the other executives in there wouldn't let me smoke. As soon as Ray would come into the box, though, I'd say, "Ray, want a cigar?"

"Sure, Jack," he'd say. We would both light up, and nobody would say a word. Ray was a hell of a guy, and he took care of his employees.

All kinds of interesting people passed through San Diego during my time there—from Jerry Coleman to Tony Gwynn to Dick Williams to Chub Feeney to Larry Bowa, who I replaced as manager in 1988. I know at that time in 1988, I said I would never manage in San Diego, but the ballclub came to me and was in a fix. I came back for the club, and we did all right.

Again, sometimes you say some things in this game and it changes due to circumstances. It's like politics. They may say they are not going to raise taxes, but then all of a sudden they do when they need the money.

As for Bowa, I always liked the guy. I hired him in San Diego as manager in 1987. I thought he was just what the club needed. We struggled and finished 65–97 that season and then in 1988 got off to a 16–30 start. Chub was the president of the club. He was the one who decided to replace Larry. He called me one morning and said, "I'm dissatisfied with Larry and I'm going to make a change."

Knowing he was an ex-Giant, I figured he had some Giant in mind to manage. I asked, "Who are you going to make the manager?"

He said, "You."

"How much time to I have to think about this?"

This was at 9:00 in the morning. He said I had until 2:00 in the afternoon to get back to him.

So I checked with my family and said, "I'm taking a lot of heat. I have nothing to lose, anyway. I've got to go down there and turn this club around."

I didn't give Larry a very good team that first year, and I told him that. In fact, I told him that if he finished 16 games under .500, he would have had a hell of a year.

I know what Chub was up against, too. It's not easy replacing a manager. I was involved in a couple of those situations. Jerry Coleman, who is the nicest guy you'd ever want to meet, a tremendous war hero, and a great broadcaster, had to be replaced.

Frank Howard and Steve Boros, two other classy guys, had to be let go. And Dick Williams got us to the World Series in 1984, but there was a change there, too.

When you manage, you can't beat the feeling of competing every day. That's why we do it. I loved to compete against Larry when he was managing the Phillies, and the games between our teams were always interesting. He's still the same fiery guy that he was when I hired him in San Diego, that's why I like him. People say this and that about Larry, but deep down he cares so much about the game. And he is a very smart baseball man. He has great work habits and is a very intense individual. He's a guy that made himself into a great big league ballplayer when people didn't think he was going to get there.

He dedicated himself to work hard to become the All-Star shortstop that he became, and he expected his players to have the same drive. Sometimes when I was in San Diego, I would say to him, "Larry, everybody doesn't have what you had. They don't have that desire.

You've got to understand that everybody can't be like you. There are guys who don't have that intensity."

Sometimes Larry gets carried away when he doesn't see that kind of intensity, the same kind of fire that he showed, and sometimes I do the same thing. I get upset with some of these players and their attitudes. But I've calmed down a bit through the years, I've tempered it a bit.

I've learned through experience that there are guys who can never have that kind of desire, there are guys who can never think like the other players do. There are guys who are not going to have work habits like other guys do.

The Padres were 16–30 when I took over in May of 1988, and we went 67–48 the rest of the way. It was nine years since I had last managed. I was ready to get back in the action. That's just the way it is. You want to be around this game every day and compete.

This game gets in your blood, and you don't want to leave. Every day you see something great and you are around such fascinating people. People always ask me what record I think will never be broken. I tell them Cal Ripken's streak of 2,632 consecutive games played. No one will ever match that. I recently had the chance to speak at a function with Cal, and he has so much class. His record just goes to show you what a competitor he is and how tough he was to play through all the injuries.

I'm sure Cal will make a great manager someday when he wants to get back in the game. This guy battled through all kinds of adversity. He's not like some of these modern-day guys who, if they get a scratch or don't feel right, are not going to play.

My favorite is, "I need a day off."

In this game, you never want to take a day off, that's why I admire people like Curt Schilling. Look what he did against the Yankees in

Game 6 of the 2004 ALCS, getting his ankle sutured to hold a tendon in place so he could go out there and pitch. Look what he did in the World Series.

That's what this game is all about. When I hear that a guy needs a day off, I say, "Are you kidding me?" Guys like Ripken and Tony Gwynn, you couldn't get them out of the lineup. You've got to love this game. You've got to want to play. Your competitive nature has to take over and you have to play through minor aches and pains, and sometimes big aches and pains.

That's what I love about the Marlins. We have some tough guys who play through all kinds of aches and pains.

I don't like it when a player is looking for an out. If you are seriously hurt, fine—but minor stuff, come on. I learned the hard way that you never ask out of the lineup.

I played a game I'll never forget in Greenville, Alabama, my first year in baseball. If we had 130 games, I caught 120. I caught every day, and Vern Law's brother Evan Law was the backup catcher. He and I roomed together. Down in Alabama it was 100 degrees every day. I lost some weight that year, but I still played every day, even though at one point I pulled muscles in both legs. I didn't want out of the lineup. We had a Sunday doubleheader, and it was hot. I caught the first game and started the second game. We were getting beat 13–2 in the third inning.

I was hurting, couldn't run a lick. Finally, the manager, Walter Thauser, took me out in the fifth inning of a seven-inning game. I went into the clubhouse and took a shower. A couple of the relief pitchers had been knocked out of the game, so they were showering, too.

I said to them, about the manager, "He knows I'm hurting. I don't know why he didn't get me out in the second or third inning."

Well, I shouldn't have been complaining. Who was standing behind me as I said that? Old Walter. He didn't say a word. He was standing outside the shower smoking a cigarette, and he heard everything.

The next day, I wasn't in the lineup.

So the day after that, I went to him and said, "Skip, I'm fine."

I learned a valuable lesson. Never complain. Sometimes your mouth can get you in trouble. Maybe that's why I'm sometimes better off sticking a cigar in mine.

Still, there are some things I wouldn't mind changing about the game. I've seen about six thousand baseball games through the years, so you know I have an opinion.

There is too much emphasis on statistical analysis. All the stuff they have today, I save that stuff for my fireplace. When I decided to pitch Josh Beckett on three days' rest, all I heard about was the record of pitchers in the World Series on three days' rest.

The writers came up and said, "Do you know that past history shows that pitchers pitching on three days' rest in the postseason are 6–20?"

I didn't give a damn about that. This was a totally different situation. None of those guys was Josh Beckett, who was on a roll. I told them all that stuff was in the past, I wanted to go forward. I'm always looking to go forward.

Hell, if you go by all that paperwork, why do you even need a manager? Let the public relations guy or the traveling secretary fill out the lineup card and let them sit up there in the press box and look at their computer and tell us in the dugout when to make changes and everything else.

Then there is interleague play. A lot of people like it, a lot of people don't. I'd make one simple change. Instead of the American League team having the designated hitter at home, I would let them have the

DH on the road in the National League parks. That way, National League fans would get to see a different style of play with the DH. And in the American League parks, I would let the pitchers hit, so the fans there could see something they usually don't get a chance to see—pitchers hitting, more substitutions, double switches, and all that.

It would make the game a little more interesting.

But I wouldn't screw around with this game too much. It's like a good cigar. You light up, sit back, relax, and enjoy the moment.

CHAPTER 16

Family Affair

My three greatest loves are baseball, my wife, Carol, and our family, not necessarily in that order. I've been lucky enough to be around baseball and Carol for more than 50 years.

Who's had it better than me?

Carol and I just celebrated our 50th wedding anniversary. It was a great party in Elon with our family and friends. Just looking around at everyone and seeing how happy they were that day puts this whole thing in perspective.

First of all, I think Carol has been able to put up with me so long because I've been away so much. Our not being together for those entire 50 years has really helped make this a strong marriage.

Carol and I met at a ballpark. What'd you expect? The opera?

I never would have met her if I didn't get thrown out of a game, so you could say umpires are good for something. And I didn't get thrown out just for arguing; this was the darndest fight you ever saw.

I was hitting, and the catcher kept tipping my bat with his mitt. And the umpire let him get away with it. The ump was Art Talley, and I was playing for Burlington. I told Talley, "If that catcher tips my bat again, all hell is going to break loose. You got that?"

So, what happened?

On the next pitch, that damn catcher tipped my bat. "I'll fix him," I thought to myself. The next pitch came in, but instead of striding toward the pitcher, I moved back toward the catcher. He was coming forward, I swung, and *bam*! I got him good, right in the mask.

I missed the pitch, but I hit my target. The catcher went down like he was shot, and the ball hit the ump right in the chest protector and bounced away for a passed ball. Our runner scored from third. Of course, the catcher and I got in a fight after that; right there at home plate, and I whipped him pretty good. Talley threw us both out of the game.

I went to the clubhouse, showered, shaved, cooled off, and went to sit in the stands to watch the rest of the game. I didn't sit just anywhere— I saw this beautiful gal, sat next to her, and started up a conversation.

She immediately recognized me and said, "Oh, you're that rowdy player."

It was Carol, and she had me pegged right from the start. Maybe that's why it took a while before she warmed up to me.

After that I used to see her at lunchtime downtown, and we eventually started dating. We got married October 29, 1954, after the season, of course. The next season I started managing.

I spent 17 seasons as a minor league manager and played 10 years in the minors. I managed 2,269 minor league games and won more than half of them. Four times I was Manager of the Year in the minors and twice in the majors. That's why winning the World Series was so special for Carol and me. She's been there every step of the way.

After winning the World Series, I said I'd never felt that excited in my life. I was more excited and proud for Carol, the kids, and the grandchildren because they'd suffered through a lot of years without a husband, father, and grandfather around. Everybody always sees the championship celebration, but they don't see all the nights you are away from your family. That's the thing about baseball that makes it so difficult, so when you do get a championship, you celebrate with your family.

This really was a family affair.

I always say the baseball wives are the unsung heroes of the game. They're the one who listen to you complain about the umpire or the manager or the players. They're the ones who hold your hand after a bad game, don't say a word, and are just there for you. And then when you become a manager or a coach, they're the ones who are babysitting your kids while you're babysitting the ballplayers.

The road trips, the late hours. It's difficult. I spent much more time with my grandchildren than I did with my own children. And it wasn't just during the season that I would be away. When my kids were growing up, I'd manage during the season, and then in the winter I'd manage in Puerto Rico. I was away all the time.

One time I had this pitcher whose hair was so long it was ridiculous. He made Johnny Damon look like he had a crew cut. During his windup, his hair would get in his eyes and he'd throw the ball in the dirt. Finally, I had had enough. I told him, "It's either the barber or a fine."

He took the fine because his wife wanted him to have the long hair. Once I found that out, I kind of understood where he was coming from, because these women put up with so much stuff.

And believe me, the players can put their wives and girlfriends through some tough times. One time when I was managing in the minors, this gal called me and said, "Has my boyfriend bought me the diamond ring he promised?"

I didn't know what to say, so I said, "Honey, how am I supposed to know?"

"Well," she said, "he told me he had to check with you first."

I felt bad for the girl. I don't know how that worked out, but I've always checked with Carol first. She has always been my inspiration.

I knew we were on a great roll with the Marlins in 2003 because right before the playoffs started, Carol went to Atlantic City and luck was on her side. Carol loves Atlantic City the way I love baseball. She was walking by the $5 machines and just had a good feeling.

She had never played them before, but she was going for it. She put two $5 slugs in there and hit for $5,000. Imagine that. Ten dollars and she hit the jackpot. Just like I did when I married her. Just like we did with the Marlins winning the World Series.

In 1999 Carol was diagnosed with breast cancer. That was tough because I was away managing the Reds. I flew home for the operation. I tried to keep her spirits up, but there were some tough times. It was pretty depressing when you read about the death rate of that cancer. Like always, I prayed a lot and went to Mass every day.

I kept telling Carol, "You'll be fine."

She went through the chemotherapy. She couldn't be around big groups of people because of the risk of infection. There were times when she was getting a little scared because some of the blood tests did not come out right, and I'd say, "Don't worry, Carol, somebody misread the thing."

Then they'd call back and say, "It's OK."

I prayed a lot and it all worked out. It really was a miracle.

Carol and I have nine grandkids. They're great kids, every one of them. There's Zachary, Braylee, Mallory, Avery, Berkeley, Presley, Kellan, Kortney and Kenzie. You can see there are some Ks in there, I'll explain that later.

You might have seen it—when my cell phone rang after we beat the Cubs for the pennant. I was on national TV, and I heard the phone ring. I was in the middle of a press conference, but I checked the number and told everybody to hold on. I answered the phone, and it was my granddaughter, Braylee, calling to congratulate me. She told me she loved me and I said, "I love you too, Braylee. I'll call you back later. I'm doing an interview."

Everybody got a kick out of that. I'm blessed to be able to do something like that. My dad was more of a "tough love" kind of guy, and his bark was louder than his bite. I guess I was that way with my kids.

We have four children: Kristi's the oldest; and then there is Kori, our other daughter; and our sons Kelly and Kasey. As you can see, I named my kids with *K*s long before Roger Clemens got the idea. If you didn't know, the letter *K* represents a strikeout in the scorebook. It's baseball shorthand. So anytime you see a *K*, that means strikeout.

Roger got his Ks on the mound. I was the other way around. I got K'd—I struck out a lot. I saw it written somewhere that I only hit 25 home runs in nearly 3,000 at-bats. The most I ever hit in a year was eight with Class C Missoula in 1958. My lifetime batting average was .210, so believe me, I know all about Ks. I thought it was a perfect way to start the kids' names.

No matter how tough it got, the one thing I always preached to my kids was to hang in there, be tougher than the situation. Sometimes they were too tough for their own good.

I remember one time my son Kasey, when he was 11 or 12, hurt his wrist playing football. He taped the wrist, put a pad over it, and continued to play. He was in a lot of pain, but he played.

Kasey didn't know any other way. He wasn't about to take himself out of the lineup. That's not the McKeon way. Well, he kept playing and he kept hurting until one day the coach came over to Carol and said, "Mrs. McKeon, I'm going to take Kasey to see the doctor if you don't. I think there is something wrong with that wrist."

So Carol took Kasey to see a nurse who lived down the block. She didn't like the looks of it either, and it turned out the wrist was broken. Another time Kasey played a baseball season with bone chips in his elbow. His brother Kelly threatened to beat him up if he left the lineup.

Kelly is six years older than Kasey, and when he was in high school he hurt his knee returning a punt. That day, he said he heard it tear, but he thought to himself, "If Dad were in the stands, he'd want me to walk off the field."

I was in Oakland managing, but Kelly tried to walk off and collapsed. He refused to go to a doctor and said he would be at practice Monday. I tried to give him a pep talk, saying, "You'll be fine. You'll be playing next week."

Instead the knee swelled up as big as a watermelon, and the coach had to take him to the hospital because Kelly refused to go on his own. It turned out that he had to have surgery, and it took a full year to recover. Doctors said he was lucky to walk again.

That's just the way this family is, it's a macho thing. We always say, "We McKeons never get hurt." We don't want anybody to pull a Wally Pipp on us.

Who was Wally Pipp? He was a Yankee first baseman a long time ago. The team won three straight pennants with him at first, but one day in 1925 he complained of a headache and sat out. He was replaced by Lou Gehrig, who played the next 2,130 games.

You see what I mean?

Whenever I was managing in the minors and somebody got hurt, I'd run out and spit tobacco juice on their wrist or wherever they got hit with the ball. It wasn't pretty, but it got the job done. It's amazing how many guys shook off their injuries when I started spitting on them. I'm surprised they didn't run the other way when they saw me coming out of the dugout. After all, who wants to get tobacco juice spit on them?

I was tough on my kids, but they're all the better for it. I used to make Kelly take 250 swings a day, and one day I even beaned him while pitching batting practice to him. I knew he had trouble with the inside pitch, and I guess I went too far inside on him. He was all right, though.

I was managing in Wilson, North Carolina, in 1960 when Kristi, our first, was born. A year later, I was still managing there when Kelly was born. I was managing at Atlanta in Triple A in 1964 when Kori was born. Kasey was born in 1967 when I was scouting with the Twins. The next year I was managing again, this time at High Point.

All my kids have been around the game their entire lives. In the summers, the boys would be my batboys.

Kelly's direct, just like me. He never beats around the bush. He'd tell you just what he was thinking, even when he was a kid. He knows the game and the lingo. There once was this pitcher named Billy Champion, who had a pretty good record, but didn't have great stuff.

Kelly went up to him one day and said, "Billy, what's your record?"

Billy said, "Fifteen and three."

Kelly looked at him and said, "You? You're kidding me."

He was only six. Like I said, he was direct, just like his father.

Another time I was managing an exhibition game in High Point and I wanted to take a look at three different pitchers. So each guy was going to get three innings. My second pitcher lost his control early and started walking people and throwing wild pitches. But I left him in there to get the work.

Six-year-old Kelly, who's my batboy, looks over at me and says, "Skip, you better get him outta there. He's walking the ballpark."

Kids learn fast, especially around the ballpark. They fit right in, and the players like having them around as long as they don't get in the way. I remember one of my players in San Diego, Tim Flannery. He was the most popular Padre of all time. If I ever traded him, I would have been run out of town. After he was done playing, Tim managed in the Padres system. He brought his young son, Danny, with him for a few weeks in the summer.

Later I saw him and said, "Flan, how'd it go? How'd Danny like being with you?"

"Jack, he had a blast," Flannery said. "He learned a lot, maybe too much. He'd eat dinner with the guys in the clubhouse. When we got home, we're all sitting around the dinner table one night and he tells my wife to 'pass the bleeping salt.'"

Another time in High Point I held a team meeting to lecture the outfielders about missing their cutoff men. We were missing them left and right, and one guy had a real problem with it, a guy nicknamed Greenie. I singled him out in the meeting, saying "Greenie, you gotta hit the cutoff man."

We went out and played and one of the outfielders, Jimmy Clark, missed the cutoff man. Jimmy knew he had made a mistake, I didn't say a word to him when he came back to the dugout. I didn't have to, Kelly took care of it.

Kelly said, "Jimmy, you're just like Greenie."

Kelly was just as hard on himself when he played, and he's still got strong opinions. One year when I was GM of the Padres, he got all over me for not signing Tim Raines, who was a free agent.

"You guys are going to stink without Raines," he said. "Go get him."

I always thought you couldn't work hard enough. When I was growing up, I was always playing baseball and jogging or doing something like hanging off tree branches to strengthen my wrists. That was just my way. My father organized the "McKeon Boys Club," so we were always playing games. I had baseball on the brain night and day. In high school, I'd play for St. Mary's, then turn my uniform inside out and catch a city league game. Then I'd go over to South River and play another game at 8:00. I couldn't get enough baseball.

I finally learned a lesson from my two boys: I expected so much out of those guys because of my background, because they had been around the game. I expected them to make adjustments quicker than other kids. When I would go out and work with Kasey, and he couldn't do the things that I wanted him to do, I'd get irritated with him and give him hell. Then, three years later, all the instruction that I was giving him fell into place. What I realized is that the mind and the body take a certain amount of time to catch up to each other.

I think a lot of parents need to know that, and this is not just about baseball or sports, it's about letting the kids grow up at their speed, not the speed you want. I had to learn that. Now with my grandkids, I realize that.

Hey, I'm still tough on the grandkids. I don't like mediocrity. I'm going to push them to get the most from their talent levels, just like I manage my players.

I'm tough, but not as tough as I used to be. Even though I may have been too hard on my kids, we've been lucky. All our kids are great. Carol gets the credit for doing such a good job raising these kids and making them such outstanding people. Sometimes I was only home six weeks a year. The job fell on Carol's shoulders.

And wouldn't you know it? Kristi married a ballplayer, Greg Booker, who pitched nine years in the majors, a guy I once traded. He went on to become the pitching coach for the Padres. He and Kristi own a family entertainment center in Elon, where you can play laser tag. Their son Zack is a pitcher-catcher at the University of North Carolina–Wilmington.

Another grandson, Kellan, has a wrestling scholarship at Duke. He won state championships his junior and senior years in high school. After he won his second title, he told me, "Hey, Papa, I just went back-to-back. I want to see you go back-to-back."

As you can see, the grandkids are competitive, too.

Kelly is living in Reno, Nevada, where he is a director of marketing and research for a pharmaceutical company. Kori is a nurse in Burlington, North Carolina. Kasey's an assistant to the general manager of the Colorado Rockies, working for Dan O'Dowd. Kasey really knows the game and will make a great GM some day. I think my own kids didn't realize what the game really meant to me until they were grown up and saw the success I had with the Marlins.

Jack Etkin, a writer with the *Rocky Mountain News* in Denver, talked to my son-in-law, Greg, and that is exactly what he said Kristi told him. She said, "I didn't realize this was so important to my Dad when I was 8 or 10 years old, but now I'm nearly 44, and I can see how important it is and how much love he has for baseball."

I think winning the World Series later in my life was so much more special than if I had won it in the seventies, instead of when I was in *my* 70s. This way, my whole family can appreciate it. Carol, the kids, and all the grandkids have enjoyed this to no end, and that's what made it extra special for me.

Sure, I love this game, but not nearly as much as I love my family.

CHAPTER 17

Playoff Magic

When I left the Padres, I wound up scouting for the Reds, and I made sure to stay in touch with Joan Kroc, just to see how she was doing. She no longer owned the Padres, but she was still keeping up with baseball. She used to tell me to tell Reds owner Marge Schott, "Get out of it, get rid of that club. They're not going to treat a lady well. They don't want the women in there. Tell her to get out like I got out, I'm enjoying it more now."

One day Joan and I were talking, and she said, "You know, Jack, I've been out of it a few years now, and I've come to the conclusion, you were the only one telling me the truth. My key executives weren't always telling me the truth."

"Well, Joan," I said, "I wasn't on the inner circle where I could get to you."

She said, "The rest of them were all telling me what they thought I wanted to hear."

That was good to finally hear. Like I said, I tell the owners the truth. Joan passed away on October 12, 2003. She was 75, three years older than me.

The day she died, we were down three games to one to the Cubs. A lot of people thought we were done. So, what happens? We win the final three games to win the pennant.

The whole postseason was like that. In the best-of-five Division Series against the Giants, we lost the first game 2–0 and were trailing 4–1 in Game 2, but came back to win. Then we got a big break in Game 3 when Jose Cruz dropped Jeff Conine's fly ball in the eleventh. We were losing 3–2 and Pudge Rodriguez won it for us that inning with a two-out, two-run single. We made the most of the breaks we had.

Those kinds of things happen in baseball. After that game the writers asked me about the fly ball. I told them, these guys are all human. They are going to make mistakes. I know you guys, you writers probably never made a mistake in your spelling or anything like that. But these guys do make a mistake once in a while. It's the breaks of the game. We were fortunate. But we also made the plays."

When the series ended, I lit up my victory cigar and said, "I've never felt this good, never felt this excited in my whole life."

The fact that we had to battle down the stretch to win the wild-card had us in a postseason mindset right from the start of the playoffs. We were determined to get the job done. We didn't let anything bother us. We had a very exciting week the last week of the regular season. If there was any pressure, I think it was shown in those games with the Phillies, where it was do or die. It was either us or the Phillies who were going to end up with the wild-card, and we just went through that week very calmly. Every day was like a routine business day, and that showed me a lot about the club. We kept that same approach during the entire postseason.

After each series, the guys got better. They got a little more experienced in handling the pressure. But it all started during the last 10 days of the regular season playing the Phillies and the Braves to get the wild-card.

That first playoff series against the Giants ended with Jeff Conine throwing out J. T. Snow at home plate as Pudge made a terrific tag. Snow would have been the tying run. That was the first time a playoff series ended that way. We won 7–6, our third straight victory in the series. Again, we made the plays we had to make.

When Jeffrey Hammonds hit the single, I kept hollering in the dugout, "Come on, Jeff! Come on, Jeff! Come on, Jeff!" When I saw him get the ball on the first hop, knowing what kind of outfielder he is, I figured we had a chance at the plate. And you have to give Pudge credit, because he made a tremendous block to keep the ball in his hands. We held the ball, they didn't.

That's the way it goes in the playoffs. One play can be the difference between winning and losing. It was that way in 1984 when I was GM of the Padres. Joan Kroc's husband, Ray, wanted to see the World Series, but he never got to see it. He died before we played the Cubs for the National League pennant that year. During those playoffs, it was almost as if Ray was looking over us. That's the way I felt. And I know when Tim Flannery's grounder went through Leon "Bull" Durham's legs in 1984, Ray was taking care of us. He had to be. He loved the Padres so much.

And just like Ray was taking care of us, I'm convinced Joan was looking over me in 2003 when we battled back to beat the Cubs in the NLCS. I didn't know Joan had passed away. When one of the writers in Chicago told me Mrs. Kroc had died, I immediately thought of Ray and how we had won in 1984. I just had that feeling. Ray didn't get a chance to see us win, and he took care of us. Now Mrs. Kroc didn't get a chance to see me win, so I just knew we were going to win. I truly believed she was looking out for me—somebody sure was—especially in Game 6 when we went into the eighth inning in Wrigley down 3–0 and ended up scoring eight runs to win.

Going into that game, Juan Pierre said it right. He said, "Ninety-seven percent of the world probably wants to see the Cubs win." The Cubs were America's darlings and everybody wanted them to get rid of their Billy Goat curse. Everybody loves the Cubbies. We knew that. But just because everybody loves the Cubs didn't mean we were supposed to fall over and play dead. Just because we had to face Mark Prior and Kerry Wood in Games 6 and 7, just because we were trailing 3–0, five outs from elimination, didn't mean we were going to just give it to them.

I told the reporters all along that our players were tough. They were going to battle all the way. We didn't come to play one game. We came in to make it a seven-game series, and that's what we did. Our guys were resilient. They didn't quit. You've got to love them for that. Every day we went out there, we just tried to win that day's game. We didn't think about what happened yesterday. We didn't worry about what might happen tomorrow. The Red Sox took the same approach in 2004—that's what you have to do in the playoffs.

Everybody talks about that foul ball, the Steve Bartman Ball, as being the difference in Game 6. To tell you the truth, I didn't really pay much attention to that play when it happened. It was a foul ball by Luis Castillo. I thought the ball was in the stands, and I didn't really think it was as much of a key as it was blown up to be.

What was the problem with what the fan did? The ball was in the stands. The umpire saw that. He was right there. Whether Moises Alou could have caught it or not is questionable, but the ball was in the stands. And when the ball is in the stands, the fans have a right to catch it. I didn't think there was any interference from our angle. So I don't think that was the turning point of the game.

We made it happen. Bartman didn't make it happen.

A lot of what we did was taken away because of that foul ball. "Bartman this, Bartman that,"—I don't want to hear it. It seems like the Cubs always have an excuse for everything. Hey, it's baseball, things happen.

Don't get me wrong, I respect the Cubs' talent, and Dusty Baker, who knows the game inside and out, is a great manager. But sometimes you have to give credit to the other guy or just admit you didn't get the job done. That's the way it is. Look at this past season with the Cubs, more excuses. It's always something; now they're upset because their broadcaster Steve Stone doesn't say nice things about them. The guy is just doing his job, and he should be credited for being honest about things. Steve Stone doesn't have anything to do with what happens on the field.

Our players deserve credit for coming back in that inning. Bartman doesn't deserve blame. I never saw an inning in the playoffs like that inning. Don't forget, their shortstop missed a ball, and that could have been a double play. To me, that was bigger than what happened with the fan. That was in the stands. The ground ball was on the field.

Pierre started the rally with a one-out double, just like he got us started all season. Then after the foul ball came Luis' walk. Pudge came through again with a single, and it was 3–1.

At that point, a lot of people still thought the Cubs were going to be in their first World Series since 1945, but I believed in our guys, and then came the error on Miguel Cabrera's grounder to load the bases. That was the big play, then we got the big double from Derrek Lee that tied the game, and we were on our way. We took advantage of every break we got in that postseason. Our guys came through like they had been coming through all season.

How about Mike Mordecai's big double? I had made a double switch with Mike, and he came up and hit a double with the bases loaded in that inning. I love Mordecai, he's such an unselfish player. You have to have players like that to win.

When things like that happen you just have to believe everything will fall into place.

The mood on the bench was very confident. Give us an opening and we're going to come through, but when you are getting down to five outs to go, you have to keep your chin up. You still have to be realistic enough to know that unless you get a break, an opening, you are going to be in trouble. We got the break and made the most of it. And the break was not that foul ball the fan touched in the stands, it was that ground ball that could have been a double play.

Once Game 6 ended, I knew we were going to win Game 7. And we did, 9–6. The celebration in the clubhouse was the greatest. That victory cigar was one of the best cigars I've ever smoked. The guys were unbelievable, and they got me to my first World Series. I will be forever thankful to them for that.

Pudge told me something terrific. He said, "Jack, we love you. You have what you want. To be in the World Series. And we are going to win the World Series for you." And they did. To hear something like that from a player of Pudge's caliber is special, one of the highlights of my life.

I never had a year like that where everything went right. Derrek Lee said I had the "Midas touch." I don't know if that was the case or not, but I know the players came through for me. They're the ones who got the job done. I asked a lot of my players, and they produced. Look at the job Josh Beckett did in Game 7 coming on in relief against the Cubs after a shutout in Game 5. Those innings he gave us in Game 7 made the difference.

Beckett is a young guy, and, like a lot of young pitchers, he had to figure things out. That's the way I do it with my pitchers. In the minors, when I had Jim Kaat, he'd come on in relief during a jam and I'd flip him the ball and just say, "Figure out how to get out of this."

And that's what he did. Fifty years later it's still the same game. Pitchers have to figure out how to get out of jams.

In that Game 7 against the Cubs, Miguel Cabrera played right field so Mike Lowell could play third. Playing right field was something Cabrera hadn't done, but we needed him to do it, and he hit a three-run home run in the first inning against Kerry Wood. He made a couple of good catches out there too, but that was just another case of going with my gut, going with my instincts. A book isn't going to tell you what's going to happen, but my instincts did. I was hoping the two kids, Cabrera and Beckett, would come up big and they did.

My job is to help these guys be the best they can be, to help them win. It's like Carl Pavano said, "Jack isn't here to make friends. He will bite you in the butt if he has to."

Yeah, I'm tough on the young guys, but I believe in them, too, and that belief paid off. After we won Game 7, some writer asked me, "You said a few times that the Lord was looking out for you. Does that mean that the Lord was not looking out for the Cubs?"

This is what I told him: "Evidently, he's trying to find that goat that has the Cubs jinxed. No, he's looking out for everybody. But like I say, I have a strong belief in the power of prayer. And believe me, it hasn't let me down yet."

After we won Game 7 that also made up my mind about coming back for the next season because we had won the pennant and that meant I would be the All-Star manager for the National League the next year. That was something I always wanted to do. I take that as a gift for my family, for Carol who has sacrificed so many things the last 50 years. It was for my kids and the grandkids, too. For all those times I was away, this was a gift for them now. I was happy for them, and for me, too.

Most of all, I was happy for the players. What a tremendous group of young men. When I took over, I told them, "Guys, if you want to work hard, pay the price, and dedicate yourselves to doing all the little things necessary to win, we'll be able to play in October." And that is exactly what happened. We became only the fourth team to come back from a 3–1 deficit in the League Championship Series to win the pennant. The Royals did it in 1985, the 1986 Red Sox did it, and so did the 1996 Braves.

The Braves lost to the Yankees in 1996, though. It was a different story for us. We still had some miracles left.

In the Division Series we had to beat Barry Bonds and the Giants. In the NLCS we had to beat Mark Prior, Kerry Wood, and the Wrigley Field ghosts, and then we had to beat the biggest ghost of them all, the Yankees in the House That Ruth Built.

What I was preaching all year came true: go out there and just have fun. When I first came to them in May, it looked like they weren't having any fun. Baseball is supposed to be fun. You should do the best you can, relax, and have fun. Like Pudge said, "Jack lets us have fun, but he's tough when he needs to be. You need a good balance from your manager, and Jack had balance."

We were about to have the most fun you could ever imagine, playing the Yankees in the World Series.

CHAPTER 18

The Ring

Nobody ever had more fun in a World Series than I did. There I was running all over Yankee Stadium smoking cigars and having a great time, enjoying every minute of it. It's like Fox broadcaster Joe Buck told me. He said, "Jack, we always have fun with you because you're the only manager who tells us anything."

After my last session with the media at Yankee Stadium after Game 6, I told everybody I enjoyed the press conferences so much. "I just want to thank you guys for helping me have such a great time," I said. And I really meant it. Some writers came up to me after that and said, "You know, in all the years I've been covering sports, you're the only manager who ever thanked the writers."

I couldn't believe that.

Another writer came up to me and said, "Jack, you were a godsend. The last two or three years these World Series press conferences were so boring. You made it fun."

I even like it when one or two writers needle me. I like to give it right back, too. That's the Jersey in me. It's like I always tell the second-guessers, call me in the dugout before something happens and let me know what I should do. Don't tell me afterward. Be a first-guesser, not a second- or third-guesser.

What we had as a team in 2003 was very special. We had 25 guys who were dedicated and unselfish. They had what I liked to call a Jimmy Valvano, never-give-up attitude. And that's what I told the media every day. It's good for the players to read that about themselves instead of something else that could be bad. Make the media work for you instead of being so defensive.

It was nice to see the players really enjoy their time in the World Series—and not just the stars like Pudge Rodriguez, Mike Lowell, and Josh Beckett.

For a guy like Mike Redmond, our backup catcher, playing and winning a World Series was a dream come true. A few years earlier Mike's dad died of stomach cancer, and Mike promised him that someday he would get the chance to play in and win a World Series. He kept his promise.

That's why I say our prayers were answered, not just mine, but all our prayers, players like Mike Redmond and so many other guys, too. You hear it every year in the World Series, and it's true.

In Game 2, we were losing 6–1, and I was able to get Mike in as a pinch-hitter. He flew out, but he kept his promise to his father, he got into a World Series, and four games later he was a World Series champion. Mike later told a writer, "If I never get another opportunity to play in a World Series, I have that for the rest of my life. Jack got me in there, and he didn't have to do that. Jack was always looking out and was thankful for the bench guys."

When you see something like that, it just makes you feel good as a manager and you remember you're not just managing the team out on the field, you're not just managing all the stars, but you're managing 25 guys.

You have to be honest with your players, whether it's good or bad, you have to let them know the truth. I've always felt that way. One of the great things about winning the World Series is that you hear from so many people that you might have lost touch with through the years. You realize you had a little bit of impact in their lives.

Over time I've gotten a little smarter and shown a little more patience with people because I've got 30 more years of experience. It's the same way in regular life, people with experience who still love their jobs should be utilized to their fullest. That's what I'm always preaching.

The game hasn't changed much, though. It's still about pitching. It's always about pitching, especially in the postseason where teams see each other day after day. When you have good pitching you are going to be in every game.

That's how we won the World Series. That's why I couldn't understand what the big deal was starting Josh Beckett on three days' rest in Game 6. He's young, he could handle it. I don't think the writers would have made a big deal of Bob Gibson pitching on three days' rest or Sandy Koufax pitching on three days' rest. Gibson pitched three complete-game victories in the 1967 World Series for the Cardinals against the Red Sox.

McCarver was the catcher for the Cardinals that year. Tim says he remembers waking up in Boston the morning of Game 7 and reading the headline in the *Boston Globe*: LONBORG AND CHAMPAGNE. The Red Sox had Jim Lonborg going, and, I guess, in Boston they thought was enough, but they didn't count on facing Bob Gibson. Timmy said that headline upset the Cardinals. "We thought that was rather presumptuous and Gibby was really ticked off," he said.

Gibson won Games 1, 4, and 7. In those three games, the Red Sox scored only three runs. Gibson struck out 26 in his 27 innings. He dominated.

It's tougher to pitch nowadays because they've basically taken the inside part of the plate, which Gibson could always work, away from the pitchers today. That's one reason for so many home runs now because everybody wants the ball out over the plate. The hitters are diving in. If you come close to them, they want to go out and fight. I would love to see some of these guys have to face Sal Maglie, Don Newcombe, Don Drysdale, or Gibson. There would be a lot of fights. Those pitchers, they established the inside half of the plate. It's like everybody talks about Pedro Martinez hitting so many guys. Well, he's established the inside half of that plate. He wants it. If you're gonna pitch inside, you're gonna hit some guys—not intentionally, you just want to get them off the plate a little bit to give yourself a chance.

Starting Gibson three games in that 1967 World Series was the right move, just like it was the right move to start Beckett in Game 6 on three days' rest. When a guy has that much potential, I want to bring it out. I want them to be the best they can be. I told Beckett and the others, "I don't want .500 pitchers. I want winners."

I had to lay it on the line to them. Sure, they could have hated my guts for pushing them so hard, but that is the way it had to be. Tough love.

Beckett knows I'm tough. He said, "Jack's a fun guy to play for, but he expects a certain amount out of you, and you better deliver. If you don't give it to him, he won't even talk to you. He ignores you. But that is just his way of motivating you, that is how he is, that's his way of getting under your skin."

It helped that I had Pudge working with the pitchers, too, because they all respected Pudge. He was phenomenal all season and throughout the postseason. He always came up with big plays.

Another guy I want to mention is center fielder Juan Pierre. He and Tony Gwynn are the two most dedicated players I've ever had, the biggest workaholics and the most focused guys. They both were totally prepared every day.

You need those kinds of players to win a championship. Winning a championship is the greatest thrill in sports. Winning any championship is fun.

The first real championship any of my teams won was the Air Force Championship. Back when the Korean War began I figured I'd join the show, so I enlisted in the Air Force and was assigned to Samson Air Force Base in upstate New York.

Even though I was in the Air Force, I still found a way to play baseball. I already had a couple of minor league seasons under my belt, so I was in good shape baseballwise. I was at the base for about a week, and I saw this sign for baseball tryouts. I was thinking, "I'm in."

Baseball was always big in the military, and Samson Air Force Base had its own team. Lt. Dave Tunno took care of me because he saw I had been a pro ballplayer. He liked my style. The first thing he did was put me in charge of the ballfield. The airfield there would have been too much for me, but the ballfield was just perfect. After a little while he saw that I knew what I was doing, so he promoted me. He put me in charge of the team, too. I was right at home in the Air Force now, running a ballfield and a team. It was just like being home in South Amboy. Life in the Air Force wasn't half bad.

I wasn't just running the baseball show, I was running the intramural athletics show, too. I had important jobs like making out schedules for basketball, badminton, volleyball, handball, and all the sports we played on the base. I never did see Korea, but I did get to see Biloxi, Mississippi, and San Antonio, Texas, because of baseball and the Air Force. That was enough for me.

Biloxi was where they held the East Coast playoffs, and we all flew down there. There we were in the Air Force, and yet most of the guys on the team had never been on a plane before and some were scared to fly. Funny, how that is.

I didn't blame anyone for being scared after our trip to Biloxi. The plane landed with two flat tires, and it scared us all half to death. We still were able to play baseball, and we won and moved on to San Antonio for the championship.

The flight there wasn't much better, and all the guys were scared to fly after that. We won the championship out in San Antonio, but the guys didn't want to fly home. So I had to call Lt. Tunno and ask him if it was OK to take the train home. And that's what we did. There we were, a bunch of Air Force guys riding the train, but at least we took the championship trophy home with us.

Great pitching was there in Game 1 of the World Series when Brad Penny, Dontrelle Willis, and Ugueth Urbina combined for the 3–2 win. After the game, I came out and told the media: "We're not taking the Yankees lightly. We know they are a good club." Everybody got a good laugh out of that one, but I was serious.

I thought we were a better club than the Yankees, but because the Yankees were so good, so experienced, and played so well under Joe Torre, I wasn't about to take them lightly. And I knew they were a little beat up from their seven-game series with the Red Sox.

Before the World Series, reporters kept asking me, "Are you afraid of the curse?"

I said that's the Red Sox's problem, not ours. I'm not afraid of Yankee Stadium and curses; I'll tell you what I am afraid of: I'm afraid of Derek Jeter, Jason Giambi, Roger Clemens, Andy Pettitte, Mariano Rivera, and Bernie Williams.

We snuck up on the Yankees in that first game in New York. So even though we lost Game 2, after two games we had our split and we were heading home. I was feeling pretty good. One of the great things we had going for us in 2003 was our 10th man, the Florida fans. That's what we had at the World Series when those sixty thousand people stood up and cheered. You know as a visiting player when you hear something like that, you say, "We've got to work hard tonight or we're in trouble."

Game 3 we took a 1–0 lead, but it just didn't work out for us and we lost, 6–1, same score as Game 2. At that point, a lot of people thought the Yankees were going to roll right through us. We really didn't hit in Game 3, and you've got to give Mike Mussina and Mariano Rivera all the credit for stopping us.

When I went to the postgame press conference, people thought we were in big trouble, down 2–1. But I still felt good about my team. This is exactly what I said that night to the reporters after the game:

> We've been down 2–1 to the Cubs, we were down 3–1 and we were in the same position where we weren't hitting. We were giving up too many bases on balls. All of a sudden, it turned around. Our pitching became pretty good. Our hitting picked us up. Guys that you see out there not doing their job now, not hitting the ball now, all of a sudden, when we had to win all three games against the Cubs, they delivered. I'm looking for the same thing to happen in the next three or four games.

That's how I felt, and it turns out, that's just what happened. But it wasn't easy. We had to beat the Yankees the next night with Roger Clemens on the mound, and it took 12 innings. Roger was fantastic, and, after he struck out the last batter he faced, we tipped our caps to him and gave him a round of applause. Later, I got a letter from Roger's agent Alan Hendricks, another classy guy I've known for years. He and his brother Randy represent Roger. In the letter, Alan wrote, "The salute from the Marlins to Roger Clemens, in the middle of Game 4 of the World Series, with everything still on the line, and Roger's salute back, will always be a very special moment in baseball. That scene exemplified what makes our country and baseball so special."

That was something to see. Alan also said great things about our organization, telling Jeffrey Loria, myself, David Samson, and Larry Beinfest, "You had the guts to take the risks you needed to take in order to achieve your goals. To your credit, almost every move you made paid off handsomely. More importantly, your commitment to winning was exceptional in an era when too many teams position themselves to reach the playoffs rather than win the World Series. Having been in the game for nearly 30 years, I have never seen a better job done by a club."

Alex Gonzalez gave us that chance to win the World Series when he hit his walkoff home run off Jeff Weaver in the twelfth inning of Game 4. It was a moment I'll never forget.

When you think about it, that was the end for Weaver as a Yankee. Gonzo had only five hits in 53 at-bats when he came to the plate, but that was the story of our season.

This was another case of sticking with your instincts. This is where 50 years of experience came into play. Alex was struggling with the bat and some critics wanted him out of the lineup. I was so happy to see him hit the home run to win the game because everybody had been getting on him. But I said many times that he's too valuable in a situation where you have a tied game or you're ahead, you're not gonna take him out of the lineup. The only time I'm gonna pinch-hit for him is if we're behind and it's late in the game. This guy got 17 or 18 home runs during the season. He just fell into a rut and couldn't get out. He got out that night.

That night someone wanted to know if all these "heart attack" games could hurt a 72-year-old manager. I just laughed and said, "This is probably the seventh or eighth time that we've done this—had the lead, lost it, battled out of a tough situation, and cashed in on an opening. I mean, that goes back to Mordecai hitting a home run in the twelfth inning. This is a very interesting team. No, it doesn't drain on me. I enjoy it."

We had one more game at home, and a win in Game 5 would put us in just the position I wanted, to go back to New York and to have two chances to win the World Series. I knew who my Game 6 pitcher was going to be, but I wasn't telling anybody yet.

I was enjoying every minute of the postseason, and that meant going to the postgame parties where they set up a tent outside the stadium. Most times, managers don't go to those events, but I figured it was all part of the fun atmosphere of the postseason. Plus there was some pretty good food there, and a few nights I even went dancing. You know, just like in that Derek Jeter commercial with George Steinbrenner. They aren't the only two who can go out and have a good time.

I was going to those parties the whole postseason. The previous series, though, there weren't as many people out there so we had more room and we finished the games a little quicker. When we were leading 3–1 in the ninth inning of Game 4, I looked at the clock and it was 11:21. I said, "Boy, this is great. We get out of here early. More time to spend at the tent." Next thing I knew, it was 12:45. I said, "Oh, there goes the party. Wasted an hour right there." I joked later with the media that we had to tell our guys to get it over quicker so we could have more time to dance and play the drums. They got a big kick out of that.

That night I got home about 3:30 in the morning and was up at 7:30 raring to go. I don't know how you can get tired in that kind of situation, really. I went to church and then came out to the ballpark. It was going to be another fun night.

We fell behind again in Game 5, but scored three big runs in the second. David Wells had back problems and we took advantage. That's the way baseball is, take advantage of a weakness. That's what I always preach. We got hits from about eight different guys and built a 6–1 lead. Brad Penny came up big for us, and we hung on in the ninth when it got a little scary.

So we went back to New York just the way I wanted it, with a 3–2 lead, and I wanted to finish it in Game 6. The next day was an off day, and when they asked me who was going to start Game 6, I said, "Our Game 6 starter is gonna be Josh Beckett. We sat around, decided that we were gonna go with our best two pitchers in 6 and 7. We know that everybody wonders why, wonders why you should, wonders why you shouldn't. We figured we might as well go with our best. We're gonna try to win one at a time. We're not looking to Game 7. We're looking to Game 6."

I really meant that. I wasn't thinking about Game 7. I wanted to win Game 6 and get it over with. The next day before the game I predicted Beckett would throw a shutout. I just had the score wrong. I had it, 6–0 instead of 2–0 and I didn't want to jinx myself. But just like in the San Francisco series and the series against the Cubs, I knew we were going to win three in a row to end it. Three was our lucky number.

In that last game I had two guys warming up in the bullpen late, but I had no intention of taking out Beckett. After the eighth inning, I talked to Pudge, and he said, "Jack, don't take him out."

"Don't worry, Pudge. Those two guys are only up for show. I'm having some fun."

I sure wasn't going to take Beckett out with a shutout. Beckett has that mystique. With him, every time out you feel you are going to win. He talked the talk and he walked the walk. He's got the guts of a burglar. He's mentally tough. And I knew he had the confidence to go out there and do the job that he did in that game.

The World Series was something I will never forget. Jeffrey Loria gave me a new sports car, a black Mercedes Roadster, at the start of the Series. It's a great car, but you can't get any luggage in it. I sure appreciated the car, but what I really wanted was that ring.

Joe Torre said no one in baseball deserved to win a championship more than I did. That was great to hear. Joe has always been a class act. He said, "I'm happy for Jack. He's a lifer." Joe's a lifer, too. He didn't win a world championship until he came to the Yankees in 1996 after a lifetime in baseball, and he knows how it feels. Joe, though, was a lot younger than me. He was just a kid, winning it all for the first time at the age of 56.

My favorite comment, though, came from Juan Pierre. During the Marlins' celebration in Yankee Stadium, he said people can call me Grampa if they want, but they also have to call me something else: World Champion.

I like the sound of that.

At the start of the next season we got our rings. Each ring looks like the rock of Gibraltar. It was the first championship for Mr. Loria, and he decided he really wanted to make something special. He had seen some other rings and decided we were going to make this the nicest and biggest ring anyone has ever received for winning a championship in any sport.

It's a beautiful piece of jewelry, and it really symbolizes my dream of winning the World Series. It's big.

It fits my finger and my personality perfectly.

CHAPTER 19

Letters from Home—Plate

You can't believe the letters I get, it's amazing. One of the most satisfying things about winning the World Series when you're 72 is that it gives others hope that they can accomplish anything they put their minds to. So many people have written me to tell me that I gave them hope. It was a blessing long after the last out was made in Game 6 at Yankee Stadium.

Here are just some of the letters that really touched me. You might recognize the name of that first guy who wrote me.

Dear Jack,

I've always thought you were one of the best people in baseball, and to see you do what you did at your age and with what you've been through, I am very happy for you and your entire family.

You deserve nothing but credit and I applaud you.

Best Regards,
George M. Steinbrenner

*   *   *

Attention Jack McKeon,

I love your devotion to St. Theresa for the simple reason I didn't think there was another man who felt the same devotion to St. Theresa that I do.

When I was a little boy my mother was devoted to St. Theresa and she used to tell me that St. Theresa will watch over me. And she did. I was in the infantry, and I can account for three times St. Theresa saved my life. Somehow my mother knew every move I made overseas. She said she communicated with St. Theresa. She knew when I was in the hospital overseas and when I was coming home. . . . When I came home she told me we have to go to St. Theresa's Church because my mother had promised her a dozen roses if I came home safe. We went to the church and put the roses at her feet and I looked into St. Theresa's eyes and I swear to you she looked down at me and smiled. That's only one story. There's plenty more miracles that happened to me. . . . If I ever meet you I would shake your hand and be proud of it.

God Bless You Jack,
Louis Bartolomeo

*   *   *

Dear Mr. McKeon:

I like to believe that you struck a blow for how effective and wise "seniors" can be. As a senior citizen, I truly admire how you showed the sports world that someone in their seventies can be a real winner. I also think you were treated in a shabby way by the Reds.

Sincerely,
Greg O.

*   *   *

Oct. 23, 2003

Dear Mr. McKeon, Manager,

We employees here at the Salvation Army in Boston are hoping you will beat the Yankees. Please win for all Red Sox fans.

In 2001 when the Diamondbacks were playing the Yankees we sent Mr. Bob Brenly a short note also, and guess what . . . it worked. They went on to win the World Series. So now we are sending you a short note in hopes it will work for you.

Go Marlins!

Sincerely,
Kathy Gould

*   *   *

Dear Mr. McKeon,

Since last May when I heard that you became a manager of the Marlins and a great deal of emphasis was placed on your age, I immediately empathized with you. Jack, I retired from retirement at age 71 and accepted a part time position at our local university 16 years ago. I am still there (age 87). It has been the calling of my life and I see that you are at that point, too.

Kindred thoughts, I am
Lillian Krieger

*   *   *

Dear Coach McKeon,

I would first like to say that I am a NY Mets fan, but the acknowledgement to Roger Clemens when he struck out your player and your whole team in the middle of the game rose to their feet to applaud one of the game's great pitchers and competitors, I think that says a lot about you and your players as individuals. I hope it sets an example for other teams in all sports to follow. This IS only a game.

Thank you,
Tom Bayard

*   *   *

Dear Mr. McKeon,

I don't know if you remember, but in early December I sent you a letter requesting that you send me an inscribed baseball card of yourself for my grandson Ben who is a big Marlins fan. You graciously did so and this is a short note to tell you what happened.

I took the card to a sports store on Long Island and after looking at it they made a 13-by-15 inch plaque for me. Across the top of the plaque was a team picture of the Marlins. Below it on the left was the score of each game of the 2003 World Series. Below it on the right, separately enclosed in plastic were two baseball cards, one of "Pudge" Rodriguez and the other of Josh Beckett. In the bottom center, between the two cards, was your card, which you had inscribed "To Ben, Good Luck, Jack McKeon."

We gave our gifts on Christmas Eve and when Ben saw the plaque he was overjoyed. When they left to go home he gave me a hug and said it was the best present he ever got. Thanks again for helping to make an unforgettable Christmas for a 9-year-old boy and his 73-year-old grandfather.

Herman Gallati

*   *   *

Manager Jack McKeon,

Congratulations on your tremendous year. . . . I am a Yankee fan but you out-managed the competition. I saw you had a quote, "St. Theresa has always taken pretty good care of me." My life has been devoted to St. Theresa since I played football at S. Cecilia High (Carmelite Friars and coached by Vince Lombardi) in Englewood, NJ. I have had a number of experiences where St. Theresa saved my life.

In World War II I was scheduled to go with a fighter squadron, but they changed my assignment and that squadron eventually crashed in the Pacific. . . . I swapped flight assignments with a friend and his plane crashed. . . . I was on a corporate jet that arrived in NJ 1½ hours early. The next day (one hour later in flight time) the plane crashed. I have had two operations in the past 16 months and was twice near death. St. Theresa made the difference. I am 84 and feeling great.

Sincerely,
Thomas P. Maher

*   *   *

Dear Jack:

I have waited until the flood of mail, undoubtedly sack after sack, has been delivered congratulating you on your fabulous success as manager of those amazing Florida Marlins. All during the playoffs when the excitement was nearly overpowering, I would calmly state that I had broadcast while you managed the Dallas–Fort Worth Rangers so I was sure that you would succeed.

It was one of the most exciting and memorable playoff series I can remember. And watching you manage and your players perform was a rewarding experience. God, I love this game. I can't believe that I am five years older but I know I must be 'cause I couldn't jog with or without a cigar. Great to know one of the game's best. . . . Manager for Life not just Manager of the Year!

Yours,
Bill Mercer

*   *   *

Jack,

Many thanks for being a terrific host. . . . I can't imagine that anyone has had a baseball career more rich in variety than yours. What a story about Branch Rickey offering you the managing jobs. The two of you have been in pro ball for a substantial portion of its existence. Congratulations on the world title. . . . And don't let anyone chase you up a telephone pole.

Best wishes,
John Lowe
Detroit Free Press

*   *   *

Dear Mr. McKeon,

Congratulations to you, Jeffrey Loria, and to all the Marlins players for winning the World Series Baseball Game on Saturday evening, October 25, in N.Y. . . . Here in our convent in Boston, a number of Sisters and myself were rooting for the Marlins to win, and praying for this outcome.

When the Red Sox played, I wanted them to win because they have been so long without a World Series victory. However, since that was not to be, I then favored the Marlins. On Saturday night we were making our Retreat and so I did not watch TV, though I would have liked to see the game. However, I thought it well to forego this desire and offer it up until the next morning. . . . On Sunday morning early, I went to check the *Boston Globe* sports pages and was so elated to see that the Marlins had won. . . . What a marvelous story is yours! . . . So inspiring and heartwarming, given that you have so much trust in God's help and the power of prayer. I have been telling the Sisters here all about you and I had to smile at your words to your players when you said: "Relax and have fun. No one thinks that we will win."

The story of your life would make a marvelous movie. I hope you will write your autobiography. I am sure it would prove to be a bestseller.

Sincerely in St. Paul,
Sister Mary Paula Kolar, fsp

*   *   *

Dear Mr. Jack McKeon,

I have been a New York Mets fan my whole life, but as I have grown older I have learned to appreciate the game. . . . There was more to the Marlins last year than just talented young players. The team circled around its manager. . . . Being a young baseball player myself, I hope to one day have a coach like you. At one time during spring training I was able to listen to you on WFAN, a New York radio station. It was a breath of fresh air to hear a voice that seemed to make much sense during baseball's troubled times, with steroids a big issue. . . . I thank you for your time and I hope you will continue to manage.

Sincerely,
Peter Link
Student and baseball fan

*   *   *

Dear Mr. McKeon,

I live in Cedar Rapids, Iowa, and am a huge Marlins fan even though it is hard because I live so far away. It was hard for me to cheer and talk openly about you guys when they played the Cubs because I live so close to Chicago.

(The 2003) season was awesome, after you took over, of course. . . . Once you guys made the playoffs I knew you were going to go all the way. A lot of people probably say that, but I actually did. . . . I listen to you, watch you on TV and read interviews you give and think you are the coolest manager ever. . . . You may be 73 but you are young at heart and in your mind. . . . Plus you are wise beyond your years, when you started Beckett on 3 days' rest in the World Series telling people to take their stats about pitchers on 3 days' rest and shove it, that was awesome and a stroke of genius.

Cheering from afar,
Chad Kleopfer

*   *   *

Dear Mr. McKeon,

Thank you so much for taking the time and going out of your way to get the autographed baseball to my grandfather. When I received it for Christmas, I squealed like a small child! . . . I work for a small recreation department with programming for senior citizens. Not only are you an inspiration to me, but I see you as a motivator to other active adults. Your humbleness and appreciation for the opportunities you have received are also reminders to everyone of how we should be thankful for what we have.

Thank you,
Iris C.

*   *   *

Dear Mr. McKeon:

First I want to thank you for signing the two baseballs for me a couple of weeks ago at the YMCA. They were Christmas gifts for my father and my nephew. I often read this summer of how the number one thing in your life was your relationship with God. I want to tell you how the Lord used you without your knowledge.

On Christmas Eve just before my parents were going to church, my mother was having a hard time breathing. She asked my Dad to take her to the hospital to get checked out. While there my mother suffered a major heart attack, which proved to be fatal on New Year's Day.

On Christmas Day, while mom was holding her own, we as a family attempted to have as normal a Christmas as we could for the kids. We gathered at my sister's house for lunch and to open presents. My nephew was really surprised with the baseball and began showing it to everyone. I then gave Dad his to open, the smile on his face was huge. He was like a little kid; it was the highlight of the day for him.

As a Christian, I believe that God works in mysterious ways. Your act of kindness provided my father with a time of happiness during a very trying time. Someday that ball will be mine and I will always be able to remember the happiness it brought to my father on that Christmas Day.

Thank you again for taking the time to sign those baseballs.

Sincerely,

Lee Pardue

*   *   *

Dear Mr. McKeon:

I'd like to tell you about a man. Alfred Lopez was born in a country where baseball is played on every street corner, grew up to play amateur baseball and dreamed one day of being able to attend a pro game in the United States. He liked the Yankees; hey there was no other team like them.

Then one day South Florida got the Marlins. The old man's dream came true. He was now living in Miami and WE got a baseball team. Hey, forget about the Yankees. He went with his wife to almost every game they could afford. They would pack a small snack, wear their aqua shirts, and watch the games.

Then the World Series was in town and this man and his wife wanted nothing more than to see the Marlins play the big game . . . however tickets were sold in a blink of an eye.

. . . At every win of the division, conference and the series; they were probably the oldest ones in Hialeah blowing their car horn on 49th Street and celebrating like teenagers. Then this Saturday, Oct. 25th, it was the old man's 73rd birthday. Thank you Marlins for one of my father's greatest birthday presents ever.

Mary Machado

I even heard from another Sunshine Boy, USC coach Rod Dedeaux, who nicknamed me Tiger.

Tiger,

When my boy Prior was knocked out of the Championships, I was loudly and clearly rooting for you, as was I think, 90 percent of the whole United States. Knowing you, it was no surprise to me, to understand that you would captivate the true followers of baseball throughout the land . . . both on and off the field. It is an honor to call you a good friend.

Cordially and FIGHT ON!!!
Rod Dedeaux

Those are just some of the letters from the sacks of mail I received. There also was a letter from a young man named Shannon, who sent his message to my good friend Joe Lutz. Shannon never really knew his father, but he grew up in the community center in Joe's town and went on baseball trips. Shannon grew up to become a New York City police officer in the Bronx. Joe and I are both proud of what he has accomplished. Shannon wrote and told us how the police department is ever-changing since 9-11, and he sent me an NYPD patch, adding, "This is a memento for coming into New York and beating our Yankees."

There also were the kind words of North Carolina broadcasting legend Add Pennfield. We became friends back when I was a young catcher. He used to catch for Duke. In 1980 he asked me to help him get World Series tickets for a local American Legion coach, Charlie Robbins, who was being honored. I was able to do that, and Add never forgot. When we went to the World Series, Bob Williams, a columnist in Asheboro, got wind of the story and wrote all about it. Somebody mailed me the story.

In the story, Add said, "I think Jack sort of does things in a way that older people appreciate. He doesn't get excited . . . [he] sort of knows things will work out."

Bob Williams then wrote: "Sort of like when one good baseball man helps another snag some hard-to-get World Series tickets. Or takes an upstart baseball team, adds a little senior leadership and cooks up a champion."

Then there was this letter that came to me all the way from Japan. It arrived just at the start of the World Series. Written on the back of the envelope were these words: "To be read before game six or seven of W.S."

I read it before Game 6.

Dear Mr. McKeon:

I have a message for you, a very encouraging one. I heard of what you said about St. Theresa helping your team because of your prayers, and I believe it.

I have been a missionary for 31 years in many countries and 15 years in Japan. I played four years of high school baseball and still follow it. Almost every year in the last 15 years or so, God speaks to me in dreams or His Voice in my heart and He tells me who will win the World Series and the Super Bowl. He has never been wrong. Last year when the Angels were in third place, I saw the Angles win the World Series in a dream.

In Game 5 against the Cubs, you lost and went back to Chicago down 3–2 games. The Lord spoke to me these words: "The Marlins are going to beat the Cubs, and they are the only team that has the fight to beat the Yankees."

I am not a Marlin fan, as I was hoping the Cubs and Red Sox curse may be over. But I believe in the voice of the Lord, and even though the Yankees are heavily favored to win, it will be a beautiful miracle when you do. It will be a battle, but I believe you can do it.

Sincerely, (In name of Jesus)
A True Believer

Then there were these two letters I got soon after I was named manager of the Marlins. This was five months before the Marlins became champions.

Dear Jack,

May the Lord give you peace. Congratulations on being named the manager of the Florida Marlins. When you want results always go to the pros. I smiled at the comment that you were 72 years young and have lots of experience but you do not work miracles. . . . Jack, I think the Marlins will get more than they think. They are looking for a good baseball man and have one but you will also bring a wonderful example of faith and goodness to the players.

In Him,
Brian Cullinane OFM Conv

*   *   *

Dear Mr. McKeon,

I am writing to tell you how pleased we are to see you back as a major league manager. Our son Sam died of cystic fibrosis 13 years ago this week. A few weeks before he died, on April 25, 1990, he threw out the first pitch at a Padres–Cubs game. You took a great deal of your pregame time to talk with him and show him around the clubhouse. We have never forgotten your kindness, which gave Sam such joy in his last days. No need to write back. I just wanted you to know we are Marlins fans now.

John, Jane & Steve Ploetz

Now you see why these letters have touched me in a way that is hard to describe. Here's one final letter that is special. Again, you may recognize the name.

Nov. 19, 2003
Dear Jack,

Congratulations on your well-deserved NL Manager of the Year Award. It truly could not have been given to a better person. It was a pleasure and honor being a part of your guidance. We could not have done it without you. Enjoy your off-season with your family and hopefully I can once again enjoy next season with you.

Respectfully yours,
Pudge

As it turns out, Pudge Rodriguez wasn't our catcher in 2004. He moved on to the Detroit Tigers, and we missed him. But all the players, coaches, front office people, and I will never forget the contributions he made to the Florida Marlins. As an old catcher, I am certain of one thing: we could not have done it without Pudge.

CHAPTER 20

Building Tradition

I was a lucky man in 2003. I had 25 guys bond together. That's what managing is all about.

I never had a team like that before in all my years of managing—minor leagues, major leagues, wherever I was. I never had a group that was so unselfish. I preached it so much, and to their credit, they listened. I told them how we could win. Everybody had to chip in. Players couldn't go their separate ways if we were going to win. I harped and harped on that.

The next year was a little more difficult. It's not easy to repeat, because guys don't have the same career years as they had the year before. A lot of teams make the mistake of thinking that just because a guy has a career year one year, he's going to have another career year the next season. It doesn't happen that way. In Kansas City, I took the club over, and we finished second for the first time in their history. I said to the general manager, Cedric Tallis, "You've got to make some changes." He said, "No, we've got a great team."

What happened? John Mayberry got hurt the first half of the season. Amos Otis got hurt, and that made a big difference. We lost two of our key hitters. It's hard to come back from that.

I knew going into the 2004 season that it would be tougher. Everybody did. When you lose a Pudge Rodriguez, that's a huge loss, and so was Derrek Lee. Both those guys are great defensive players, too. Everybody knows about Pudge and catching, but an under-looked aspect of the game is defense at first base. In 2003, Derrek must have saved us about 50 errors. He made all the plays. At first base, you have to have good, quick hands and quick feet, that's the key.

Despite the loss of some great players, I knew there was still a good enough nucleus here. We were deep in pitching, and we all felt we could be serious contenders again. I came into spring training with the idea that we were going to win this thing.

Teams like ours, the Cincinnati Reds in 1999, can still be in the hunt if they've got the right players. It's not the money that gets you there, it's the players. You can have medium-priced players that are good, better than high-priced guys. It's not the salary, it's the type of player you have.

Right from the start, I told the team we had to work harder because we had some holes and we lost some offense. There was less of a margin for error. Going in, I thought the league had improved, and right from the start I said Atlanta was not going to go away. The Phillies have a lot of talent, but that team just never seemed to click.

The most difficult thing for us was trying to get the offense going, sometimes we didn't make adjustments and sometimes I think we were trying too hard. As a consequence, it snowballed.

The whole key to a successful offense is having hitters who take the pressure off of one another. In San Diego, we got Steve Garvey to take the pressure off of Kevin McReynolds. We got Graig Nettles to take the pressure off of Tony Gwynn and Carmelo Martinez. If you got in a tough ballgame, a 3–3 game with the winning run at second base, Garvey would get the hit. Then McReynolds or Martinez came up behind him, and they hit because the pressure was off.

Anytime you have a young club, you need a couple of veterans around them to take the pressure off. The kids will follow the leader of the veterans. That's the key. That's what guys like Mike Lowell, Pudge, and Jeff Conine did for us in 2003. We didn't always get the big hit the next year.

Our pitchers have done a great job, and that is the backbone of this club, guys like Josh Beckett. When I was with the Reds, pitching coach Don Gullett and I would sit in the dugout, look over at the Marlins talent, and say, "Wouldn't we like to manage that club?" They had some raw talent over there that was just about to mature.

The Florida organization did a great job accumulating so much talent. And fortunately, I was able to manage the club I wanted to manage. It was like a miracle. When I got in that room in front of the players for the first time, I told them: "Hey, we have enough talent in this room to win. But it's all up to you. If you want to pay the price, I'll show you how to do it. It's not up to me, it's up to you. How bad do you want to do this?

"We have enough talent to get to the playoffs. Here's what we have to do. We've got to dedicate ourselves; we have to work a little harder; we have to have a much better focus; and most of all, we have to play unselfish baseball and have fun. I want you guys to have fun. I want you to enjoy coming to the ballpark every day. And I want you to play relaxed. When it's fun coming to the park, you'll play much better baseball."

I needed to impart the winning knowledge to the young guys, especially the pitchers—Beckett, Penny, Pavano, Willis. I tried to get inside their heads, and when a mistake was made, I would go down the bench and explain things.

And when things were done well by someone, I would point it out, too, even if it was the other team, like a pitcher going short with two strikes, learning when to throw a ball. Another pet peeve of mine is letting the big guys beat you by making a mistake. Give them a single, give them a walk, but don't let them hit the ball out of the ballpark late in a close game. Just constantly talk baseball. They were eager. On a lot of teams, that's been lost.

People say to me, "How do you stay so calm?" I may look calm on the outside, but I'm hot on the inside. I can't show them that I get disturbed because they messed up. Because then the rest of the guys will look at you and think, "Geez, what happens if I screw up."

And that works in any business. If I get pissed, I raise hell on the bench every once in a while, but not as often as I would years ago. I've matured. I learned that when I came back from San Diego. I've learned to have more patience and to not let the little things bother me. File it, and at the right time, bring it up. Timing is key.

I don't have many team meetings, but I do have one when necessary. A week after I first took over, I had a meeting in L.A. We had lost four in a row, and I didn't like the way we played. I closed the door and let them have it, I said, "I'm not here to be a caretaker, I'm hear to win. I'm not happy with the lack of effort we are putting forth."

So what happened? We went over to Montreal and lost three more. But then we came back to Cincinnati, won three, and started to roll.

They had to understand that I wasn't happy to just be there, I was there to win and they found that out quickly. I could coast and sit back, but I wanted to win. I cared about them.

It's also so important to make moves to show them you care. Larry Beinfest, our general manager, did a fantastic job adding talent in 2003 and 2004. In my opinion, he's been General Manager of the Year the last two years. He's a great guy to work for and very dedicated. I wasn't surprised at all when *Baseball America* named us the Organization of the Year in 2003.

Before the 2002 season, Larry traded for Dontrelle Willis. Then during the year, he added Juan Encarnacion, a player we lost after the 2003 season and then got back for the stretch run in 2004. Larry also traded for Carl Pavano, a great deal with Montreal. Then before the 2003 season, he traded for Juan Pierre and signed Pudge. I've made a lot of deals in my days, but those are special moves.

Every time we were in a position where we could have gone downhill, Larry and his people went out and got a player. They went out and got Ugueth Urbina. They got Chad Fox. Mike Lowell got hurt while we were in a heated battle with the Phillies. We lost a guy with 32 home runs, but then, they went out and picked up Jeff Conine. That gave a tremendous boost to our players, and they came through in the clutch. When you have a chance to win it, you go for it, even if it takes away prospects you may be counting on in 2007. Go for it now. Live for today.

That's what we did. We made the moves that enabled us to win it all in 2003 and gave it our best shot in 2004. Picking up Paul LoDuca and Guillermo Mota really gave us life in 2004, but it didn't work out like the previous season for a lot of reasons.

Still, we had to grow as a team, and I think we have.

I had to put a little reminder on the board the last week of May during the second game of a series against the Reds. I put up this note: "To whom it may concern: Check your egos at the door. We won last year with 25 guys playing as a team."

That's it.

It was just a gentle reminder. I wanted to reinforce what we are. We're a team, we're not a bunch of selfish players. It was aimed at just a couple of guys. They are good kids, but sometimes they have to be reminded that it's a team game and not to show up anyone.

To me, that's when ego gets in the way a little bit. If you're blasting a teammate or someone in the organization, you are not thinking about the team, you are thinking about yourself. So that was the perfect timing for a little note.

I never like to point fingers directly at individuals. Whenever I have a meeting with my team, this is how I handle it—and I think this is good advice for any team meeting, in sports or business. I say, "Now look, there's a lot of stuff I'm going to say. It doesn't apply to everybody, but if the shoe fits you, wear it. And I hate for some of you guys in this room to have to hear this stuff, it doesn't apply to you, but for the ones it does, listen up and take care of it."

That way you get everybody's attention and you don't make anybody defensive by calling them out in front of their teammates. You get your message across to the people you want to get it across to and you don't embarrass anyone.

I was proud that we had a winning season again in 2004. We finished in third place in NL East with an 83–79 record. After finishing as World Champions, there's a lot of pride there, and I didn't want to see us go down the tubes. These guys battled all season, and it was nice to be part of the only back-to-back winning seasons the Marlins have ever had. I always like to try to get guys to overachieve, but I've been lucky here. We really have good guys here, guys who want to go out and give you everything they have. Some have enough, some don't.

At least you know one thing: you're going to go out there and get the best out of them. I think we really represented ourselves well, and I'm excited about 2005.

I'm not the type who wants to hear, "We won last year. That will hold us over for a while." I want to win every year. I don't believe in making excuses, either. So that's why, even though we had a rough schedule in September 2004, I didn't want to make a big deal out of it. We were doing OK until Hurricane Ivan got us. Mother Nature got us. No team in major league history has had to face a schedule as grueling as ours was the last month.

Who would have thought we were going to get strapped with three doubleheaders in 11 days when we didn't have a doubleheader scheduled all year, and then lose our ace? We also learned something else, don't ever underestimate the Braves. They've won 13 straight divisions.

The way I look at it, it's not like another team knocked us out of the playoffs. If anybody knocked us out of the playoffs, Hurricane Ivan, or as I like to say, Hurricane Pudge, did. That hurt more than anybody.

Maybe it wasn't meant to be that year. Now if Hurricane Pudge had come in 2003, that really would have hurt. But we had nice, sunny weather. The Good Lord was looking after us. This past year I think he said to me, "You got your reward last year. You have to wait."

As Charlie Finley used to say, "Don't be a hog."

So we tried to make the best of it. That's why when we had some games rescheduled for Chicago at U.S. Cellular Field, I didn't want to make it bigger than it was and give the players an excuse to lose. So when the writers asked me what it was going to be like to be playing "home" games in the town of the Cubs, a team with whom we were fighting for the wild-card, and playing in an American League park, I just said, "I imagine we'll have a lot of White Sox fans and a lot of Cubs fans who will come over there and root for us."

When Hurricane Frances came through Florida, a lot of us stayed at the ballpark, Pro Player Stadium. We spent four days together there. We had the big-screen TVs, spaghetti dinners, hot dogs, and the sauna. We had all the comforts of a country club. They even brought in a cook for us. It was almost like a five-star restaurant.

And we were very lucky there. We never lost power. We made the best of it. That's what you do. We sure felt bad for the people who got hit hard. We're just playing a game. We felt bad for our fans and the people who lost so much to the four hurricanes—people who lost their lives and people who lost their homes.

The thing about Florida is that it is such a caring community. That's why I love managing here. I can't begin to tell you how many close friends I've made here, people who will help you in so many ways, people like Norman Rales, who has done so much to reach out and help people he doesn't even know and never wants any credit for it.

I know ownership wants to reward the fans and put a contending team out there every year. Jeffrey Loria is interested in building tradition. He's a winner. He promised the people that he would do everything possible to put a winning team out there, and I think he has shown that by the extra effort he has made in expanding payroll, making trades during the season to improve the club, and making sure players like Mike Lowell will stay with the Marlins. Mike is a class act in the clubhouse and in the community. You have to have players like him to succeed and to build tradition.

I've been in a lot of organizations through the years, and I love the way this organization is run. They back you 100 percent. That's not the case in a lot of other places. There are a lot of people that have a part in winning: the players, of course; but scouting and player development is so important. It's a winning attitude across the board.

It looks like there's going to be a new ballpark soon, and that's something the people of Florida can really be proud of. It gets back to what I was saying before, building a tradition, not just a ballclub. All that makes me want to stay here. I need to manage two more years to move ahead of Casey Stengel and become the second-oldest manager in Major League history. That would take me through the 2006 season, and that would make me 76.

I'll probably feel about 49 then. I've been blessed. I owe so much to all my players, coaches, front office people, and owners through the years. There's been so many outstanding organizations. I really appreciate them for helping me to accomplish my dream these last 55 years.

I know the players are going to keep getting younger, and I'll be getting older, but I'm not worried about any of that. I've had my best success with the young guys. Why should I stop now?

Hey, like these kids, I'm just getting started.

Jack McKeon's Managerial Record

Year	League	Team	G	W	L	WP	Finish
1973	AL West	Kansas City	162	88	74	.543	2
1974	AL West	Kansas City	162	77	85	.475	5
1975	AL West	Kansas City	96	50	46	.521	2
1977	AL West	Oakland	53	26	27	.491	7
1978	AL West	Oakland	123	45	78	.366	6
1988	NL West	San Diego	115	67	48	.583	3
1989	NL West	San Diego	162	89	73	.549	2
1990	NL West	San Diego	80	37	43	.462	5
1997	NL Cent	Cincinnati	63	33	30	.524	3
1998	NL Cent	Cincinnati	162	77	85	.475	4
1999	NL Cent	Cincinnati	163	96	67	.589	2
2000	NL Cent	Cincinnati	163	85	77	.525	2
2003	NL East	Florida	124	75	49	.605	**Won WS**
2004	NL East	Florida	162	83	79	.512	3
TEAM TOTALS		Cincinnati	551	291	259	.529	
		Florida	286	158	128	.552	
		Kansas City	420	215	205	.512	
		Oakland	176	71	105	.403	
		San Diego	357	193	164	.541	
TOTAL			1,790	928	861	.519